BEFORE WE KILL AND EAT YOU

H. B. Garlock
WITH RUTHANNE GARLOCK

Regal

From Gospel Light
Ventura, California, U.S.A.

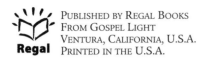

PUBLISHED BY REGAL BOOKS
FROM GOSPEL LIGHT
VENTURA, CALIFORNIA, U.S.A.
Regal PRINTED IN THE U.S.A.

Regal Books is a ministry of Gospel Light, a Christian publisher dedicated to serving the local church. We believe God's vision for Gospel Light is to provide church leaders with biblical, user-friendly materials that will help them evangelize, disciple and minister to children, youth and families.

It is our prayer that this Regal book will help you discover biblical truth for your own life and help you meet the needs of others. May God richly bless you.

For a free catalog of resources from Regal Books/Gospel Light, please call your Christian supplier or contact us at 1-800-4-GOSPEL or www.regalbooks.com.

Originally published by Servant Publications in 2003.
New edition published by Regal Books in 2005.

Map illustration by Lloyd Colbaugh.

Library of Congress Cataloging-in-Publication Data
Garlock, H.B., 1897-1985.
 Before we kill and eat you : the miracles and adventures of a pioneer missionary couple in Africa/H.B. Garlock with Ruthanne Garlock.
  p. cm.
 Includes bibliographical references and index.
 ISBN 0-8307-3907-6 (trade paper)
 1. Garlock, H.B., 1897-1985. 2. Garlock, Ruthanne.
 3. Missionaries—Africa—Biography. 4. Missionaries—United States—Biography. I. Garlock, Ruthanne. II. Title.
 BV3505.G27A3 2004
 266'.0092—dc22   2004000106

1 2 3 4 5 6 7 8 9 10 / 12 11 10 09 08 07 06

Rights for publishing this book in other languages are contracted by Gospel Light Worldwide, the international nonprofit ministry of Gospel Light. Gospel Light Worldwide also provides publishing and technical assistance to international publishers dedicated to producing Sunday School and Vacation Bible School curricula and books in the languages of the world. For additional information, visit www.gospellightworldwide.org; write to Gospel Light Worldwide, P.O. Box 3875, Ventura, CA 93006; or send an e-mail to info@gospellightworldwide.org.

DEDICATION

To the grandchildren and great-grandchildren of Henry B. and
Ruth E. Garlock, who follow their example of faith as Christ's
representatives in the earth.

CONTENTS

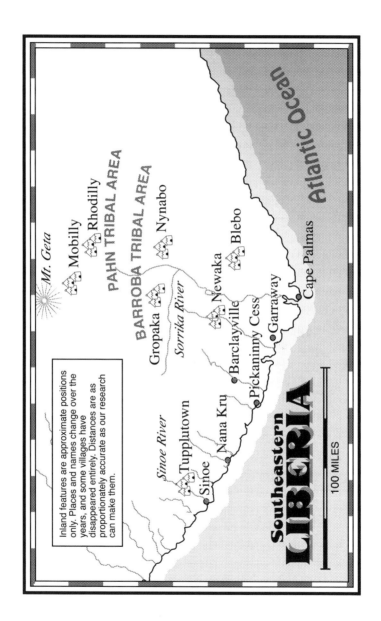

Inland features are approximate positions only. Places and names change over the years, and some villages have disappeared entirely. Distances are as proportionately accurate as our research can make them.

Mt. Geta

Mobilly

Rhodilly

PAHN TRIBAL AREA

BARROBA TRIBAL AREA

Nynabo

Gropaka

Sorrika River

Newaka

Blebo

Barclayville

Pickaninny Cess

Garraway

Cape Palmas

Atlantic Ocean

Sinoe River

Tupplutown

Nana Kru

Sinoe

Southeastern

LIBERIA

100 MILES

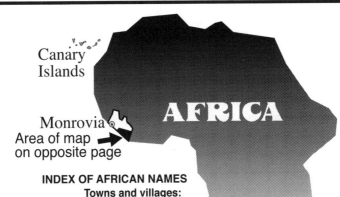

Canary
Islands

Monrovia

AFRICA

Area of map
on opposite page

INDEX OF AFRICAN NAMES
Towns and villages:

Mountains and Rivers

Tribal Groups

FOREWORD

Few Americans in any era have known Africa as Henry B. Garlock has known the continent. He was one of the last of a breed of missionaries who entered and survived by the power of the Spirit alone. What he experienced in Africa could well be an additional chapter to the Book of Acts. His experiences read like legend.

H.B. and his wife, Ruth, invested their lives in Africa. They prowled the jungles before there were roads, airfields, radio or telephone communication, or military protection. They lived in aboriginal housing, battled malaria, and saw others cut down before they had started. They faced the raw power of wickedness, intertribal warfare, cannibalism, the incantations of hell, and the gloom and despair of centuries of superstition.

But the repeated breakthroughs God provided made it worthwhile. What the Garlocks learned the hard way could be passed on to those who followed them to Africa in increasing numbers. Scores of missionaries have been able to say, "Ma and Pa Garlock touched my life. Garlock's counsel to me, and interest in me, saved me from blunders. He really introduced me to Africa."

A man like Garlock would never be content to do a mundane day's work. He was not a hireling or an institutionalist. There was the intrepid in his soul—that element that makes the truly great missionary. His answer to God's call took him far beyond the comfortable and the ordinary, down paths where no line of retreat was kept open. He repeatedly placed himself in circumstances where God would have to reveal himself in authority, or he would never leave the situation alive.

Fortunately, my great friend was gifted with an abiding sense of humor that has been a God-used component in his life and ministry. You will chuckle as you meet the very real characters and experience the very frightening situations through the eyes of a man filled with God's peace and an abiding love for Africa.

You will be proud that God has had men such as this author. It is a simple narrative, for H.B. Garlock was a simple man. What he did for God and the gospel he thought it his duty to do.

I believe this book will be a call to others as they read, and that H.B. Garlock's investment in souls will be multiplied. I know he has influenced my life.

C. M. Ward
Revivaltime radio broadcast speaker for the
Assemblies of God, 1953 to 1978

INTRODUCTION

My first introduction to H.B. and Ruth Garlock was in April of 1964, in Springfield, Missouri, soon after I had become engaged to their son, John. They had come to attend an international conference of ministers, and John was eager for me to meet them. I knew his parents had served as long-term missionaries in various parts of Africa, but at that time I had no idea just how remarkable their experiences had been.

They immediately put me at ease and made me feel welcome in the family. I faced quite a challenge in marrying John, because it meant taking on the responsibility of his two daughters, then eight and thirteen years old. Their mother had died suddenly following a brief illness the year before, and John, Linda, and Melody had moved to Springfield where I was working on the staff at Central Bible College. Shortly after our wedding the following summer, the elder Garlocks warmly received the four of us at their home in Bakersfield, California, when we drove out for a get-acquainted visit.

Over the years my relationship with Mom Garlock became especially close. People often commented about the irony of our names being so similar. Her name was Ruth; she had named both her African daughter and her natural daughter Ruth; now her son's bride turns out to be Ruthanne! In innumerable ways, but particularly in regard to missions and full-time ministry, she was like a mentor to me. Her love for God's Word and her strong faith never failed to encourage and inspire me, and I now cherish the many notebooks I have filled with her sermons and Bible lessons.

Both Mom and Dad Garlock were living repositories of African lore and amazing stories about their experiences in Africa and in other far-flung places of ministry. But always the emphasis was on thanking God for his faithfulness to bring them through even the most impossible situations.

In 1973 John and I moved to Dallas, Texas when he was named director of Christ For The Nations Institute, and his parents came to visit us there. When CFN cofounder Freda Lindsay learned that their stories had not been published in book form, she insisted that Christ For The Nations should do this. Since I was on the editorial staff at the time, I got the assignment to create a manuscript from the raw material of Mom and Dad Garlock's diaries, magazine articles, and recorded messages. The first edition of *Before We Kill and Eat You* was released by CFN in November 1974.

Now, twenty-eight years later, I have the opportunity to re-edit this timeless material and enrich it by adding a few quotes and additional stories—especially stories from Ruth's unique experiences. I have been humbled and amazed all over again to see how God protected and provided for these two young zealots who followed his call to Africa. Mom Garlock used to say, "We didn't feel we were doing anything particularly remarkable—we were simply doing what we felt God wanted us to do, and he blessed it."

Though advanced in years and contending with health problems, Mom Garlock never lost her missionary spirit. She was an eighty-nine-year-old widow when she learned I was leading a volunteer team on a missions trip to an orphanage in Haiti.

"Please take me with you," she said. "I want to be a missionary one more time." She and I had a great time being roommates on that trip, and she was an inspiration to everyone in the group. Her assignment was simply to sit in a big rocker in the orphanage playroom every day to cuddle and rock the dozens of infants, toddlers, and preschoolers, and pray over each one of them.

Dad Garlock was a favorite speaker for inspiring people to catch the vision for world missions and to dedicate their lives to help take the Christian gospel to the ends of the earth. Countless numbers of missionaries have gone to the field because of his influence. Others, when disheartened, have been encouraged by his example to remain faithful to their call. He was fond of closing a missions message with a quote from Reverend George P. Howard—words which sum up the essence of their motivation:

We have a humanity that is too precious in the sight of God to neglect; we know a remedy for the ills of the world that is too wonderful to withhold; we have a Christ who is too glorious to hide; we have an adventure that is too thrilling to miss.

Everyone who became acquainted with Henry and Ruth Garlock quickly learned that they embraced the adventure of missions ministry in Africa. They withheld nothing, but rather were grateful that God gave them the privilege to serve him as they did. As you read these pages, may their story of faith encourage you to trust God completely in obeying his guidance for your life.

Ruthanne Garlock
November 2002

ONE

RESPONDING TO THE CALL

And when he brings out his own sheep, he goes before them; and the sheep follow him, for they know his voice.

JOHN 10:4

U nder normal circumstances, I would have been thrilled to get a letter from home at mail call that afternoon. But my heart sank as I scanned Mom's message. At last, after years of praying and hoping, my dream of enrolling in Beulah Heights Bible School to prepare for the ministry had come to pass. And now, after only two weeks of study in North Bergen, New Jersey, came the desperate plea, "Henry, please come home."

Because I was the eldest son of twelve children born on a farm near New Haven, Connecticut, my father took me out of school from time to time to help with the work required to feed such a large family. By the time I was fifteen, I had to quit school completely. I helped my father on our own farm, and also worked for various neighbors to help bring in some income. Finally, at the age of twenty-one, I had left home to attend Bible school.

I slowly reread the letter. Father and some of the other children were ill with influenza; no one left at home was able to work. Would I consider coming home to help just until Father was able to go back to work? The job I had previously held was still open for me. "Anyway, please do pray about the matter," Mother pleaded in closing.

With a heavy heart I prayed through the night, struggling to make the right decision. And in my memory I relived the earlier events of my life as I sought God hour after hour.

Through the years my mother and brothers and sisters and I knew what it was to go hungry because Father sometimes spent every cent he made for liquor. His addictions and violent temper caused much grief for all of us. On the other hand, Mother had experienced a genuine encounter with the Lord, and her godliness greatly influenced the lives of all her children. She took us to a Methodist church, where at the age of eleven I went to the altar and accepted Christ as my Savior.

When I was sixteen years old we heard that Maria Woodworth-Etter, a well-known evangelist at the time, was conducting a tent revival in the area. Mother bought a train ticket to Long Hill, Connecticut, and gave it to Father. "I want you to go to that meeting and stay until God does something for you," she told him. "Don't come back home until you're changed." He did as she requested.

A few days later while I was working outside, I heard him singing as he walked up the path to the house. My first thought was, *Sounds like Father is drunk again.* But he wasn't drunk at all—he was singing a gospel song and praising God. He gathered Mother and all of us children around him in the parlor and told us he had been saved, healed, delivered from his addictions, and filled with the Holy Spirit. Edmund Garlock was never the same after that day. The change in his habits and behavior in the following months proved his conversion to be real.

God's Hand on My Life

Seeing the miraculous transformation in my father's life inspired me to rededicate my own life to the Lord, and I began to fast and pray, seeking to be filled with the Holy Spirit. On Christmas Day in 1913

I experienced a powerful baptism in the Holy Spirit similar to that described in Acts 2:4 on the Day of Pentecost. From that moment on, my whole life changed.

Although keenly aware of my lack of education, I hoped the Lord could somehow use me in his service. My great desire was to enter Bible school, but it seemed like an impossible dream. In 1917 I visited Beulah Heights Bible School, and later that year my sister Blanche enrolled there. But it appeared that my parents could not get along without my support, and since I was the eldest son I felt it was my responsibility to help the family.

By the fall of 1918 the United States was deep into the First World War. I was now twenty-one and eligible for the draft with an A-1 classification. While expecting to be called to the Army any day, I became violently ill with influenza in an epidemic that was sweeping the country. Most of the young men in our town who had not left for military service were stricken; within a few weeks many of them died. And as I grew steadily worse my family feared I would be yet another victim of the epidemic—more people died with influenza than were killed during the war. As I lay unconscious on the bed, my parents' only recourse was prayer. Following is the account my father recorded of my illness:

> We prayed, but Henry grew worse each day until one morning he was hemorrhaging from the lungs. I realized that unless God undertook he would die. I didn't know what to do and wondered if I should call a doctor. I took the Bible and asked my wife where I should read. "In the place where you have opened," she replied. It was 2 Chronicles 16:12b-13a, concerning King Asa: "... in his disease he sought not to the Lord, but to the physicians. And Asa slept with his fathers ..."

"If we turn to the doctor now, Henry will sleep with his fathers," Jessie said. So we did not call the doctor—we determined simply to trust God.

About sunset I went into the bedroom where Henry lay and saw that he did not breathe. I was filled with fear, but God gave me power to rebuke death in Jesus' name. At first there were no apparent results; he still did not breathe. I spoke again with no visible results. The third time as I rebuked death he opened his eyes and saw us standing at the foot of his bed.

"Yes, Lord, I'll Go ..."

As I travailed in prayer in my dormitory room and wept over the letter from Mother, I relived that awesome experience. I remembered sensing that I was leaving my body that was lying on the bed in the bedroom of our farm home. As I left the house and traveled diagonally upward, I saw a golden stairway and Jesus standing at the top of it. All my aches and pains were gone—I felt as light as a feather. At that moment I was certain I was going to be with the Lord. How long my spirit was gone from my body or how far I traveled into space, I do not know.

But suddenly a hand seemed to be laid upon me and I heard the Lord's voice call me by name: "Henry, go back!" the voice said. "I have work for you to do. If you come now you will come empty-handed. I want you to go to Beulah Heights Bible School to prepare for missionary work."

At first I was hesitant, as I now felt so peaceful and happy and free from suffering. But again I heard the voice of the Lord speaking clearly: "Go back! If you come now you will have no sheaves to lay at my feet. You must leave all and follow me. I want you to preach the gospel."

As soon as I said, "Yes, Lord, I'll go," immediately I descended the way I had come, down to the farmhouse and into the bedroom where I saw my body lying on the bed. When I opened my eyes I saw Father and Mother standing at the foot of the bed, rebuking death and the devil. There was great rejoicing in the house when they realized their prayers had been answered.

Though I had wasted away and was very frail, my healing was so complete that three days later I was able to leave home for Bible school. I feared to put off going any longer. The words of the apostle Paul, "woe is me, if I do not preach the gospel!" (1 Corinthians 9:16), had become a vital part of my life.

Only a few days after I had enrolled at Beulah Heights, the Armistice was signed on November 11, 1918, ending the war. Thus it was unnecessary for the government to induct more young men into the Army.

No Turning Back

My dear parents had cared for me and prayed for me during my illness. In fact my father, whose sickness Mother was now writing about, had no doubt caught the influenza from me. How could I be so ungrateful as to refuse her appeal? As the tears flowed, I opened my Bible and asked God to speak to me from his Word. Immediately my eyes fell on the verse in Luke 9:62 (KJV): "No man, having put his hand to the plough, and looking back, is fit for the kingdom of God."

I said, "But surely, Lord, this Scripture doesn't apply to me. It is merely coincidental that I happened to turn to this verse in the Bible. Please give me another Scripture to guide me in the decision I should make."

I opened my Bible the second time and Matthew 10:37 stood out before me in what seemed like bold, black type: "He that loveth father or mother more than me is not worthy of me: and he that loveth son or daughter more than me is not worthy of me."

I knew God had raised me from my deathbed and called me to leave all and follow him. But my parents, whom I loved dearly, were in dire need. For me to refuse to go home now to help them would be unforgivable. On the other hand, if I had died, they would have had to get along without my support. In fact, for two long years I had put off going to Bible school because it seemed my folks could not possibly get along without me. Now I was brought face to face with the issue as never before.

I continued to seek God through the early morning hours. When it was time for the morning chapel service I went downstairs and asked the Lord for one more sign from him before making my final decision. After the opening song of the meeting, the speaker of the morning announced his text and read from Luke 9:62: "No man, having put his hand to the plough, and looking back, is fit for the kingdom of God."

Without waiting to hear his message, I returned immediately to my room and wrote my reply to Mother. It was the most difficult letter I have ever written.

I told her that I loved my family more than life itself, but I knew God had called me and I dared not turn back. I shared the Scriptures God had given me during the night, and told her how these had been confirmed in the chapel service that morning. I assured her that I was praying for God to heal Father so he could return to work, or to raise support from some other source. With a sense of great relief I mailed the letter and prayed that God would meet the need.

Within a short time I received another letter from home. Mother began by apologizing for the earlier letter she had written. She went on to say she was proud of her son for deciding to follow God, and she would not have me return home for anything in the world. God had completely healed Father and he was working at a better job than he'd had before. My younger brother was now working and bringing in some support. I felt it was God's provision and blessing in response to my obedience.

The previous year, while doing extra farm work for a neighbor, I had been able to help with my sister Blanche's expenses when she enrolled at Beulah Heights ahead of me. Now both of us were thrust out into a life of sheer faith. Sometimes our needs were met supernaturally; some of the time I found temporary or part-time jobs to earn what we needed. For a while I shoveled coal at a mill a few hours a day. During another period I tended machinery in a factory. Though we occasionally had to do without some things, the Lord faithfully supplied our basic needs. When we graduated in 1920, all our financial obligations had been met.

The Call to Africa

Blanche had received her call to missionary service before I received mine. At a missionary prayer meeting one day, as she sensed a great burden for the heathen, she saw the word "AFRICA" spelled out in letters of fire. I, too, felt a special burden and love for the people of Africa, but I rather hoped God might call me to some other foreign field, since Blanche was called there. However, Africa also was to become my own call and passion.

On March 26, 1919, while praying at Bible school, I saw a vision that is described in chapter eight of this book. Its effect was to convince me beyond all doubt that God wanted me to go as a missionary to somewhere on the African continent; I did not know just where.

Shortly after seeing this vision, I heard William Johnson, one of the first Pentecostal missionaries to go to Liberia in 1908, when he spoke to the students at Beulah Heights. He told of the many unreached tribes in the interior, and appealed for strong young men who could walk the trails and withstand the hardships of the malaria-ridden country—then known as the "white man's grave." After the Lord had miraculously healed me of influenza, I had asked him to let me go to a hard field—a field where no one else was willing to go—so my heart responded to this challenge. Blanche also felt that Liberia was the place where God wanted her to go.

In my second year at Beulah Heights, Alfred Trotter enrolled as a student and became my close friend. He was almost like a younger brother to me. Alfred's sister, Ruth—a schoolteacher in Newark, New Jersey—often came to visit him. I not only met her, but also enjoyed some of the home-baked treats she would bring to her brother.

It seemed Alfred never stopped talking about his wonderful sister, and before long I thoroughly agreed with his evaluation. She was attractive, intelligent, lively, well-organized, and—most important of all—fully dedicated to the Lord. She was the youth group leader of her home church in Newark, of which E.S. Williams (later General Superintendent of the Assemblies of God) was pastor.

I was amazed to discover that this outstanding young woman also felt a call to Liberia, but neither of us placed much priority on romance at the time. I had gone to Bible school for one purpose—to prepare to fulfill God's calling. Now I had to follow that calling. But I did invite Ruth home to meet my family, and we kept in touch.

Stepping Out in Faith

After graduating from Beulah Heights, Blanche and I went home to Connecticut for a brief visit. Father thought I might want to do farm work at least for the summer to get some money together. But I took seriously the Scripture in Romans 11:29, "For the gifts and calling of God are without repentance." I felt this meant I must fulfill my calling and leave for Africa as soon as possible, while trusting God to meet my needs. I agreed to stay and work on the farm for one week, for which I was paid fifteen dollars. As far as I am aware, that was the last money I ever received for secular employment.

Blanche and I were invited by a former Beulah Heights student to conduct some meetings in Dolington, New Jersey. The people had absolutely no money to pay the one-dollar-per-night rental required for the use of the town hall, but we felt led to undertake the challenge anyway. We went about the town all day inviting people to the meetings. At night I would preach in my limited way, and Blanche would sing. Night after night, people came forward for salvation when we gave the invitation—including the members of the town council from whom we had rented the building. In the end, they refunded the money Blanche and I had paid for rent, and gave us an offering besides! It was God's way of showing us he could provide for our needs.

Next, some friends in Philadelphia invited us to come preach in a city mission, which we did. Then we attended camp meetings at Media and Export, Pennsylvania. We shared our vision and burden for Liberia, receiving much encouragement, but almost no financial support. Next, Blanche accepted an invitation to visit a friend in Ohio while I went to conduct meetings in New York state for my friend Frank Finkenbinder. (He later became a career missionary to Latin America and father of the well-known "Hermano Pablo" Finkenbinder of radio and television.)

I left Frank in Elmira, New York and boarded a train for New York City, where Blanche was to rejoin me. But God had other plans. Shortly after my journey began, I looked up and saw the sign for Owego, New York, as the train pulled into the station. Suddenly I was aware of an inner voice that said, *"Get off the train!"*

I argued that it was a foolish idea ... that I'd paid for a ticket to New York City ... that I didn't know a soul in Owego ... that I was practically penniless. It did no good. The inner voice of the Holy Spirit was loud and clear. So, just as the brakeman was shouting "All aboard," and lifting the small step from the platform, I grabbed my cardboard suitcase containing my extra collar and socks and got off the train.

Now what? I walked over to the station house and saw a poster advertising a Pentecostal camp meeting! A man with a team of horses was putting cargo that he had just unloaded from the train onto his wagon. When I asked if he knew where this camp meeting was being held, he said, "Yes," and that he would soon be going that way and could give me a lift. I accepted his kind offer and quickly reached the campground.

It was a real tent city. As I approached the large meeting tent an elderly white-haired man came to meet me. "Are you a preacher?" he asked.

"Well, I ... yes ... that is, I'm a missionary to Africa!" I blurted. I told him how the Lord had impressed me to get off the train at the Owego station, and when I saw the camp meeting poster I felt sure that this was the place I was to come.

"Praise the Lord, he has answered our prayers!" the man responded. "Our evangelist has lost his voice, and we've been praying that God would send us a preacher. Will you preach for us tonight?"

This was a formidable task for a new Bible school graduate, but under the circumstances I was afraid to say no. It turned out that my invitation was from Brother F.S. Perkins, president of the Pentecostal

Holiness Association of New York and Pennsylvania.

I spent the rest of the day in prayer, and that night stood up to preach. The large tent was filled, and it seemed there were as many people standing outside as there were inside. After a very short message (in which I felt I covered most of the Bible), I gave an altar call and the aisles filled with people coming to kneel in the straw. I do not know how many were saved that night, nor how many were healed and filled with the Spirit. I only know that I was almost scared to death.

After the service the leaders of the camp asked me to preach again the following night, and I consented. I stayed there for several days—praying throughout the day and preaching at night. And each night the altars were filled with seekers. But I soon understood why the scheduled evangelist had lost his voice. The camp was right beside the main railway line (a typical Pentecostal location in those days), and every few minutes a monster double-header steam locomotive would come through pulling a freight train to Buffalo. With no public address system and all that noisy competition, I, too, was reduced to a whisper after a few days. So I prepared to be on my way.

But by now these dear people felt they knew me, and they took a great interest in my plans for going to Africa. Not only did they give me a generous love offering, but also told me they had been keeping in the bank a missionary fund of five hundred dollars, waiting for God to send along the right person to receive it. As a result of this camp meeting in Owego, the Pentecostal Holiness Association decided to support Blanche and me financially for our first term of missionary service in Africa. Later, after each of us had married, they increased the amount of their support. How grateful I was that I had obeyed the prompting of that inner voice to get off the train!

Besides the support of the Pentecostal Holiness people, we also received endorsement from the Eastern District Council of the

Assemblies of God. Twenty-five years later I had occasion to read these remarks written by E.S. Williams in recommending me to the Foreign Missions Department: "The brother is young, but full of zeal, and I think will make a good missionary." The Assemblies of God granted our missionary appointments in the fall of 1920.

So much had happened since Bible school graduation that spring! We had met numerous other missionaries and missionary candidates. We had established a few roots among people who promised to pray for and support us. We had seen God supply the cost of our fare and basic outfit to go to the field.

Leaving All Behind

Most important to me, I had become engaged to Ruth Trotter. She was at the New York pier to see us off when the time came for Blanche and me to sail. Naturally it was hard for Ruth and me to part. But we wanted God's will for our lives more than anything else in the world, and both of us felt the call of God should come first. I would go to Liberia and get a place ready for us to live. As soon as she fulfilled her teaching contract for that school year, she would join me.

I can almost see her yet as through the tears we both waved while the ship slowly moved away from the pier and down the Hudson River. Given the dangers and uncertain conditions of missionary work in those days, we wondered whether we would ever meet again. And I had given no thought at all to raising my return fare. I was completely focused on reaching Liberia and taking my place of service there.

My mother and father also had come to New York to see us off. They were giving up two children for the mission field in one day, but they were glad to do so. Many times during severe tests in Africa, we were to feel their prayers sustaining us. And so it was that by the grace of God and the help of many kind friends, we sailed out of New York harbor on October 23, 1920, aboard the *S.S. Carmania* of the Cunard Steamship Company, bound for Liverpool, England, where we would take a ship for Africa.

The voyage took ten days. One of the highlights for Blanche and me was meeting for daily prayer and fellowship in the stateroom of fellow-passenger Paul Rader, president of the Christian and Missionary Alliance, and a well-known evangelist at the time. We maintained correspondence with the Raders for some time afterward as they visited mission stations in many parts of the world.

Our parents and friends gave us a number of dated envelopes to be opened on specific days of our crossing. Five days out I had my twenty-third birthday, and an envelope from my mother contained a poem she had written for the occasion. It seemed to me that day the most wonderful piece of poetry I had ever read:

Birthday Greetings to Henry

God bless my boy this morning
A happy, bright birthday
While on the ocean sailing
From home so far away.

Tho' far from home and loved ones
Our prayers are with you still;
We trust our heavenly Father
To keep you from all ill.

This day brings to remembrance
The one so long ago
When you a tiny baby
Launched on life's sea of woe.

The cold and snows of winters
And summers twenty-three
Have passed since that bright morning
When you were given to me.

All through the days of childhood
And boyhood's happy years,
A comfort to your mother
Through many trials and tears.

And now upon the ocean
You're nearing England's shore
And will soon be sailing
To Africa's open door.

To the country of Liberia
Into the "White Man's Grave"
To the land where Jesus calls you,
Some precious soul to save.

But He will go before you,
With you His Spirit fill.
"Lo, I am with you always"—
His promise He'll fulfill.

—Jessie Garlock (1876–1970)

TWO

THE WHITE MAN'S GRAVE

I will instruct you and teach you in the way you should go; I will guide you with my eye.

PSALM 32:8

The *S.S. Carmania* docked in Liverpool on the Mersey River at 3:00 P.M., November 1, 1920. We were met by an agent of the Edwards Brothers' Forwarding Agency, who escorted us to a reputable boardinghouse. Wide-eyed and shivering in its under-heated rooms, Blanche and I were already thousands of miles farther from home than we had ever been before. Here in England, the land of our ancestors, we would await passage on another ship to take us thousands more miles to West Africa.

We had left New York before receiving confirmed reservations for passage from Liverpool to Cape Palmas, Liberia. A great many ships had been sunk by the Germans during the First World War, making it difficult to secure bookings to West Africa. Some had advised us to wait until definite bookings were confirmed before leaving the U.S. But we felt as we stepped out in faith that God, who had called us to Africa, would go before us and prepare the way.

We were on a waiting list with a company operating freight boats and an occasional passenger boat to West Africa. They told us it would be at least a month before we could expect to get passage, and that it would depend entirely on cancellations. So we found a Pentecostal mission where we could stay while waiting.

After more than three long weeks we got word of a single cancellation on the *S.S. Ekari,* sailing the next morning. I accepted the vacancy and left Liverpool on November 24. Another ship, the *S.S. Boma,* sailing a week later, had room for Blanche and the Alexander Howards, another missionary couple awaiting passage to Liberia.

On my second day at sea, Thanksgiving Day, I rejoiced to make this entry in my diary:

> Wrote to my sweetheart. My heart is filled with praise and thanksgiving to our precious Lord for so wonderfully opening the way for me to be sailing for dark Africa on this Thanksgiving Day, 1920.

I was scheduled to go ashore at Monrovia, Liberia, and wait there to transfer to the *S.S. Boma* (which by then would have space) in order to reach Cape Palmas. But upon learning that the city of Monrovia was under quarantine because of a smallpox epidemic, I disembarked early at Freetown, Sierre Leone. I spent one week with missionaries there and had my first opportunity to preach to a group of Africans. A few days later the *Boma* made a port stop in Freetown, and I went aboard to join Blanche and the Howards. The last leg of the journey would take us to Cape Palmas, Liberia.

Brief History of Liberia

In 1817 the American Colonization Society was organized in the U.S., and in 1822 its first expedition of freed slaves arrived on Providence Island, off the coast of Liberia. From that date, freed slaves or their descendants have crossed the Atlantic in small numbers to settle on the

Liberian coast. A white American minister, who at the request of the Society went out to aid the new settlement, invented the name "Liberia" meaning "free."

After acquiring land from the inhabitants of the region, the new settlers established the town of Monrovia, naming it after U.S. President James Monroe (in office 1817–1825). Following the example of England, which authorized its men to board slave ships and release the slaves in Freetown, Sierre Leone, the American Navy was empowered to seize slave ships on the high seas and release the captives in Liberia.

Though the new community suffered from hunger and disease and many of the early settlers died, gradually their number increased. But by 1965 it was estimated that there were still no more than twelve to fifteen thousand Americo-Liberians living scattered along the coast. The tribespeople of the interior numbered perhaps one million, although no accurate census had ever been taken. Liberian independence was recognized in 1862, but the government had many difficulties both with economic management and with the hostile tribes of the interior.

Missions in Liberia

For many years Liberia was known as the "white man's grave," owing to its extremely unhealthful climate. The death rate among missionaries was so high that some mission societies decided to pull out of the country, believing it to be impossible to evangelize. Of seventy-nine missionaries sent to Liberia by the Church Missionary Society of London before 1830, forty-four died of fever during their first year of service. Of seventy-five sent out by the American Presbyterian Board, thirty-one died within a very short time and many others returned home ill.

Out of a large party of Methodist missionaries led by Bishop Taylor in 1895, only Miss Jessie Arms survived a siege of fever. In 1900 a party of ten missionaries, including Mr. and Mrs. John Perkins and Miss Arms, who was returning for her second term, arrived in Liberia. Mr. Perkins reported that after three months there were only two left—he and Miss Arms. His first wife having died, he and Jessie were married in Liberia and under God were spared to carry on the work for over forty years, despite many hardships.

While on furlough during 1907, the Perkins heard about the Pentecostal revival that was sweeping America. They attended a camp meeting and received the baptism of the Holy Spirit. With this new "equipment" they felt they were now better fitted to face the problems of pioneer missionary work in Liberia. But when they applied to the Methodist Board of Missions for reappointment, they were turned down because of their Pentecostal experience.

No organized Pentecostal missions groups existed in those days, so they returned to the field independently. Not only did God supply their fare and their outfit, he raised up six other Pentecostal missionaries to accompany them. Included in this party was William Johnson.

Mr. Perkins did not wish to be unethical by going in near the established work of the Methodist mission where he and Jessie had once labored, when there was so much unevangelized territory in the hinterland. While praying for guidance as the ship approached Liberia, he felt God gave him a vision showing him that Garraway, a small settlement thirty miles northwest of Cape Palmas, was the place where the party should go ashore.

When he told the ship's captain they wanted to be put off at Garraway, the captain replied that this would be impossible. Never had a ship stopped offshore at Garraway because of the great danger from submerged rocks. Furthermore, he faced the risk of losing his job as captain if he ventured to do such a thing. But Mr. Perkins insisted that God had spoken to him in a vision and had told them to get off the ship at Garraway.

Finally the captain relented. "If God told you to get off at Garraway, then Garraway it shall be," he said. "But you must take full responsibility for what happens to you and your party in getting ashore."

To this Perkins and the others readily agreed. So on Christmas morning, 1908, the ship anchored two miles offshore. The party of eight missionaries was lowered over the side of the ship in a "mammy chair"—a kind of square box with board seats facing each other—into a lifeboat. Some of the ship's crew then rowed the group and their baggage ashore at Garraway.

As their little boat was beached, an African man came rushing up to them. "I know who you are—you are missionaries!" he said excitedly. "God appeared to me in a dream while I was at home in the interior, telling me to come to Garraway to meet a party of missionaries who would come to my tribe to preach the gospel. Just follow me and I will show you the way to the Barroba tribe."

The story sounds like the instance recorded in Acts 10 when Simon Peter visited the house of Cornelius. He found the man's entire household ready to receive the gospel message because Cornelius had received a vision of an angel.

The party followed this man, Jasper, into the interior to the Barroba tribe and established the first Pentecostal mission station at the town of Newaka. They learned that Jasper had been converted while attending a Methodist mission school on the coast, and soon sought for and received the baptism of the Holy Spirit. He was a great help to the early missionaries, and became the senior pastor among the Barroba people.

Within a year after their arrival, almost all the members of this first party of Pentecostal missionaries, as well as the workers who had joined them, had either died or been sent home with broken health. Many a palm and breadfruit tree bears mute testimony that under the shade of its branches lie buried the mortal remains of some pioneer missionary. It is conservatively estimated that during the first twenty-five years of the Pentecostal work in Liberia, at least one missionary a year died of malaria or some other tropical disease. And many others returned home because of serious illness—among them William Johnson, who later returned to the field.

Disease also took its toll among the local tribespeople. From long marches through the forest, overexposure, and fording flooded streams and marshes while out preaching, Jasper contracted tuberculosis. (About a year after I reached Liberia it was my sad duty to bury this dedicated man of God at Newaka, alongside the missionaries already laid to rest there.)

Our Arrival

On the morning of December 19, 1920, the *Boma* anchored offshore at Cape Palmas. A surfboat flying the Liberian flag and manned by native oarsmen pulled alongside, and two Liberian immigration and customs officials climbed the rope ladder to the deck. A little later a boat brought the shipping line's Cape Palmas agent and missionary William Johnson to meet us. It was through Johnson's ministry at home that we had received our call to Liberia.

After considerable red tape, the ship was cleared for landing passengers. We, with our few items of baggage, were placed in a mammy chair and swung over the side by the ship's hoist into the waiting surfboat bobbing up and down in the rough sea below. Our mammy chair hit the rolling surfboat with a tremendous thump. With the help of many black hands that reached out to steady us, we climbed out of the chair into the tossing boat.

The experience of a new missionary landing in West Africa is graphically described by Jean MacKenzie in her book, *An African Trail,* written in the early 1900s.

Give a thought to him, as he goes over the ship's side. In the main he is young; his helmet is new against the sun. His baggage is all zinc or tin or japanned steel against the rains and the roaches and the white ants. He sits in the surfboat between the brown bodies of the rowers who line the gunwales. They sing the song of rowing; they rise and fall to the paddle with the impeccable rhythm of their race. The new man marks the incredible white of their teeth and the whites of their brilliant eyes.

His unused attention is wine to them. They shout and swing in an accelerated and measured frenzy as one man. They are the sinews of the hand that Africa has put out to pluck the white man from the deck where he stood among his brothers—those that speak his tongue and follow his customs. By that hand he will be led along what lonely paths to what foreign experiences! That black hand may become to him hateful or dear. It may crush him or it may, after rainy seasons and dry, replace him on a deck of a steamer making north. But be sure of this, the print of those fingers is upon him—the spirit and the body of him— to the end of his days. That imprint is upon him like the scar of the lion's paw on the arm of Livingstone.

To Garraway

After clearing customs in Cape Palmas we engaged a surfboat to take us and our baggage the following day to Garraway, about thirty miles back up the coast, from where the trip to the interior was to begin. There were no hotels in Cape Palmas, but I managed to secure sleeping quarters in the Methodist mission, and Blanche stayed at the steamship agent's residence.

At five o'clock the next morning, December 20, we set out for Garraway. The native boatmen hoisted a sail and we were driven at a rapid pace along the coast. At times it seemed we would be dashed to pieces on the rocks. Then there would be a calm during which the oarsmen were supposed to row, but they generally decided to take a nap while waiting for the wind to become more favorable. Mr. Johnson and Blanche were very seasick and I sang "The End Is Not Yet" to add to their discomfort. (It so happens that I have never been seasick, but I usually refrain from admitting it after hearing that only "idiots" are immune to seasickness!)

The trip on the surfboat was very trying. The sun beat down and the glare from the sea was blinding. We tried to hold umbrellas over our heads for protection. It was a relief when the sun went down, but we did not reach Garraway until 1:30 the next morning—sunburned, weather-beaten, and very tired. A day and a night in an open surfboat on a tropical sea is no picnic! And twenty hours to go thirty miles is not very fast traveling.

Garraway, which was to be our "jumping-off place" to still more primitive parts, had already been the site of much missionary sacrifice. Long before the landing of Perkins and Harrow, a Methodist station had been opened here in 1887 by a Reverend and Mrs. Gortner, accompanied by their two young sons and a Mrs. Meeker. Fever had struck them all as soon as they reached Garraway. Agnes McAllister, herself a missionary to Garraway a short time later, wrote about that missionary party:

> Mr. Gortner, his wife and elder son, and Mrs. Meeker were all confined to bed at the same time. Only the younger son and an old Liberian woman were able to do anything for the sick. Mrs. Meeker, who was well on in years and not very strong, was the first to die from the fever. It was in the afternoon. And in the evening of the same day Mr. Gortner went to be with Jesus, leaving his wife and son too sick to help themselves, or attend to burying their dead. The two dead bodies lay there until the third day before anything was done toward burying them.
>
> Some sailors, hearing of the deaths at the mission, went up and made two coffins from the board partitions of the house and buried the bodies. Mrs. Gortner, who was too sick to stand on her feet, crept on her hands and knees to take a last look at her husband. When Bishop Taylor at Cape Palmas heard the news he went to Garraway to look after Mrs. Gortner and the two boys. They recovered and returned to America.

The Fifteen-Hour Trek to Neweka

Now Garraway was once more seeing the arrival of new missionaries—but Blanche and I would not be staying. A group of porters and hammock men were waiting for us, having been engaged by Mr. Johnson to carry our loads and assist us to reach Newaka in time for the annual Christmas convention which was to begin on Christmas Eve. At Garraway we divided our outfits into headloads, and at 3:00 A.M. on

December 24 we headed for Newaka. It was a distance of thirty-five miles, normally considered a good two-day walk through dense forest and jungle.

Much of the way Blanche was carried in a hammock made of a piece of light canvas hemmed at each end, with a piece of clothesline rope threaded through the hem and tied to a bamboo pole. At each end of the pole was a strong native who balanced the pole on his head, using a rolled circle of leaves or grass for padding. Since the jungle path was very narrow the whole party had to walk single file.

The men of the caravan sang and shouted in rhythm as we traveled along. The trail was crooked, as the Africans generally detoured around fallen trees and branches rather than cut them out of the way. On the winding trail it was difficult at times to know whether the songs of the marchers came from in front or from behind. Sometimes the carriers and hammock men trotted along at a good rate, and at other times slowed down to cross streams or rises of high ground. The caravan rested briefly at intervals, usually near a stream.

In midmorning and again in midafternoon all stopped for a meal beside the trail, or in a small village. Some of the boys carried rice and a three-legged pot in which to cook. Brother Johnson shot a few monkeys along the trail to provide meat to go with the rice. It seemed that whole tribes of monkeys passed through the forest over our heads most of the trip. The foul odor at times was stifling.

Finally, footsore and weary, we reached Newaka mission station at about 6:30 P.M. the same day we had started, having made the long march in about fifteen hours. We received a warm welcome by the missionaries and native Christians who had gathered for the convention beginning that night. I recorded in my diary: "It is wonderful to be in the land of our adoption. Our first Christmas in Africa, December 25, 1920, I was asked to baptize the twenty-four candidates who were ready for water baptism. This was a great experience for a rookie missionary."

After Christmas, Blanche and I went to Blebo mission station to assist Mr. and Mrs. Edgar Personeus, arriving there on New Year's Day, 1921.

Trip to Pahn Territory

Leaving Blanche at Blebo on January 13, I returned to Newaka to accompany William Johnson on a trip to the interior. He was interested in the Pahn people, a tribe which were reported to be cannibals, and who had never heard the gospel. After a nine-day march through incredibly dense forest and almost impenetrable jungle and bush—not to mention wading through swamps and swollen streams—we finally reached Rhodilly. It was the first large village of these warlike people.

Word had reached the Pahns that two white men with porters were approaching their territory. Being forewarned very literally meant being forearmed in this case. We were met at the outskirts of the village by a group of warriors carrying cutlasses, spears, bows and arrows, and cudgels. Our caravan halted as our carriers cried out that we did not bring war or trouble, but came peaceably and would do them no harm. When they saw that we were unarmed and our manner seemed friendly, they lowered their weapons and allowed us to enter the village of Rhodilly.

This tribe had never been subdued by the Liberian government, so the people carried out their own customs and practices in the tradition of their ancestors before them. Having heard how government soldiers had invaded and subjected other tribes near the coast, they were determined to fight to retain their independence. Consequently they were very suspicious of strangers who ventured near their private domain.

Not only were we the first white men they had ever seen—we also were the first people they had ever seen fully clothed. Some of the Pahn people wore loincloths made from grass or leaves or from the bark of trees, but most of them were completely naked. Many of them wore their hair braided in numerous pencil-thick braids and all of them had their front teeth filed to a point.

We made our way to the center of the village where the chief's court traditionally was held. Most of the women and children hid themselves as the men cautiously approached us. While none of the men in our caravan knew the Pahn language, a few of them knew some words spoken by an adjacent tribe. So by relying on faulty interpretation and gesticulations, we managed to make the chief know we wanted a place to stay for the night.

At first he flatly refused our request, and some of the men cynically told us to go sleep with the monkeys in the bush. They told their chief, King Tho, that they were suspicious of us and that we should not be trusted. However, after much persuasion, which included presenting the chief with a blanket, we succeeded in convincing him that we were not representatives of the government and were not there to do them any harm. King Tho assigned huts for our little company to stay in, and after a meal consisting mostly of rice, we stretched out on our army cots for the night.

I was exhausted from the nine-day trek through the jungle, and was grateful that our party had a roof over our heads for the night. After a few hours' sleep, however, I was awakened in the dead of night by the sound of voices. I tried to look around the hut to see if anyone had entered, but a smothering blanket of darkness lay over everything. It was impossible to see, and I felt I dared not light a torch.

I lay awake staring into the blackness—wondering what these people were saying, and what I should do. Knowing they were cannibals made the experience even more frightening. But all I could do was commit the matter to the Lord and pray for his peace and power to prevail. I soon fell asleep again and the night passed without incident.

We spent several days in Rhodilly near the foot of Mount Geta, and gradually King Tho became quite friendly. He listened attentively to the story of salvation we tried to convey to him. Finally he consented to allow John Yeddah and Timothy, our two native workers from Barroba, to live among his people and tell them more about the good news of the gospel. This was a major victory of the entire trip.

With the help of some of the villagers we managed to erect a small two-room rectangular house before leaving for home. John and Timothy returned to Barroba with us in order to get their families. The Pahn people gave Mr. Johnson and me new names—Kwi Yonsini and Kwi Kali. "Kali" was as near as they could come to saying Garlock, so I became known to them as Kwi Kali, which meant "white bird."

Tragedy at Newaka

We arrived back at Newaka on February 18, having been away for thirty-two days. Mr. Johnson felt that if all went well in locating two native workers and their families in a Pahn village for a few months, it would open the way for missionaries to eventually go among them to live. It took real courage and dedication on the part of John and Timothy to volunteer to live among these primitive people.

From Newaka I returned to Blebo to join Blanche and Mr. and Mrs. Personeus. Shortly after my arrival Blanche was stricken with her first attack of malaria fever and ran a very high temperature for a week.

Many missionaries have died from their first attack of malaria. Thus it became the custom of the mission that no one was to be left alone at a station until after having had his or her first bout with malaria.

On March 14, after Blanche was almost recovered, I went to the Newaka station to put doors and bamboo shutters on a mission house. Ten days later all the missionaries and native workers were to gather there for an Easter convention. As we approached Newaka a terrible tropical storm broke upon us, accompanied with great claps of thunder and streaks of lightning. The rain came down in a cloudburst and we were soaked to the skin as we swished along on the narrow, snakelike trail.

When we reached Newaka we found that lightning had struck a huge cottonwood tree under which seven schoolboys had taken shelter while trying to keep birds off the ripening rice at the mission farm. All but one boy had been struck to the ground; he ran to the mission for help. Three resident missionaries hurried to the scene of the tragedy and managed to revive three of the boys by applying artificial respiration. But since they were unable to work on the others in time, three of the boys died. Naturally the convention began on a sad note. The first meeting was a funeral service, as it was necessary to bury the dead immediately in such a hot climate.

After the evening meeting, when all the missionary workers had retired, we were suddenly awakened by a series of weird, bloodcurdling sounds that warned the experienced missionary and native worker that "the avenger of blood" was on the march. In these primitive people's minds, no one ever died by accident or of natural causes. Some person was always held responsible for every death in the tribe.

Through a series of certain incantations, the local witch doctor had come up with the reason for the death of the three boys on the rice farm. According to him, it was some person or persons in the nearby village of Simlika who must be ferreted out and given the "sasswood test." If, after having been compelled to drink the poison brew, the victim vomited, he was innocent. But if he died, as most did, he was declared to be guilty of bewitching the deceased. The Newaka witch doctor and his men were now on their way to Simlika to demand that the sasswood test be administered to its people.

The forest path to Simlika passed the mission station, and Mr. Johnson recognized the meaning of the weird night calls of the witch hunters. He called on the missionaries and native workers to help him block the trail to Simlika. We all hurriedly dressed and followed him. As the witch doctor and his men approached, Mr. Johnson remonstrated with them, and with the help of the native Christians physically restrained their leaders until we could talk to them.

He told these men that the Simlika people were not responsible for the lightning bolt killing the boys, but that it was an act of nature. God had no doubt allowed it to get their attention and to get them to repent and turn to him before anything worse happened.

The *palaver** turned out to be an all-night session. But with God's help, this wise missionary was able to get the warriors to turn back, thus averting a great deal of bloodshed. The people of Simlika would certainly have resisted unto death the demands of the Newaka witch hunters.

By this time I had been in Liberia for less than three months. Yet the many experiences I'd had—so foreign to anything I'd ever known back home in Connecticut—made it seem as if at least a year had passed. Truly, it was almost like being on another planet, not just another continent. But I was content with the assurance that I was here in God's will to do my best to make him known to these people who lived in such darkness.

---

* From the Portuegese word *palavra,* meaning conference or profuse talk. Used by Portuegese traders on the coast of Africa, it became a colloquial expression meaning a conference or discussion, usually among tribal leaders to settle a dispute.

THREE

A TROPICAL HOME FOR NEWLYWEDS

Also I heard the voice of the Lord, saying, "Whom shall I send, and who will go for Us?" Then I said, "Here am I! Send me."

ISAIAH 6:8

While on our journey to Pahn territory, William Johnson and I had passed through Gropaka and the abandoned mission station overlooking the village. The station had been closed after the deaths of the two women missionaries who had started a work there. It was a sobering experience for us to find two graves, marked with crude markers, in a grove of trees near the compound.

Gropaka had been the farthest interior station among the Barroba tribe, and was in the center of quite a dense population. An abandoned mission station is always tragic, and my heart went out to the people of Gropaka and the surrounding territory. It appeared the missionaries who had built the station lost their lives before a strong church could be established there.

When I returned to Newaka, I asked Mr. Johnson to allow us to reopen the Gropaka station. Knowing that Ruth would join us on the field in a few months, I was anxious to have a place ready for her when she arrived. The village chief, King Jufuli, along with his elders, came to the Newaka Easter convention and begged that missionaries be sent to Gropaka to replace those who had died. How happy they were when they learned that the newly-arrived missionaries would reopen the station.

After the convention Blanche returned to Blebo with Mr. and Mrs. Personeus, with the understanding that I would send for her as soon as I could get a room ready for her to occupy in the old house at Gropaka that was about ready to collapse.

On April 13, 1921 I arrived at the abandoned mission compound to begin repairs on the premises. The house, built of hand-sawed boards, was situated near two large cottonwood trees on the highest elevation in the yard.

To build a house in these primitive conditions, a missionary must first employ some local men to fell trees in the nearby forest, which would be cut into eight- or ten-foot lengths. Then the workers would dig a pit deep enough for a man to stand upright in it and operate one end of a two-handled saw. At the top was another worker. Together the two slowly sawed the logs into enough boards for the walls and floor of a house. This tedious process normally required a whole day to get just one board sawed out. The house was elevated on posts about three feet off the ground as protection against termites, dampness, and mold in the unusually wet climate.

Unfortunately, the material that had been used to build the house at Gropaka was not termite-proof, so the white ants had eaten away most of the posts and wooden steps at the front and rear of the building. In fact, the front steps collapsed as I entered, and many of the floorboards in the house crumbled under my weight. The place seemed to be a rendezvous for rats, snakes, scorpions, and huge tropical lizards. Of course there were no glass windows, and the white ants had long ago eaten away the bamboo mats that had once been used as shutters.

Reality Sets In

I placed my army cot in one room where the floor seemed secure and hung a protecting mosquito net over it. I had been told that the net would frighten away wild animals, so there was nothing to fear. But the noise of the huge rats running across the floor at night annoyed me. The people of the nearby village sang and danced most of the night to the monotonous beat of drums. The birds' shrieking night calls sounded at times like the cries of huge monsters. And the monkeys chattered incessantly in the bush. The noise kept me from getting much sleep the first few nights. In all my twenty-three years I had never felt quite so alone as I did then. But a much more disturbing thing happened during that first week of my stay in our new home.

I was awakened in the night by the terrified screams of a small child of a family housed in a temporary hut on the compound. The boy had just stepped outside the hut when a prowling leopard pounced upon him and dragged him away into the dark. His family, anguished but helpless in the darkness, could do nothing to rescue him. All of us listened in horror as the poor little fellow's cries became more distant, then ceased. The next morning, in the high bush nearby, we found fragments of his skull and hands and feet.

This frightening experience, following the sobering jolt I had felt the day I arrived on the hill and looked at the lonely graves of the last two missionaries, banished any illusions I may have had about the glory of doing pioneer missionary work. I was now face to face with cold, stern, hard reality.

I began to wonder if I were doing the right thing to bring my sister and my prospective bride to live in such a dreadful place. But after praying and reflecting on the matter, I soon realized that both Blanche and Ruth had received their calls to missions work from God, just as

I had. They were as willing as I was to go through whatever suffering was required in order to bring the gospel to these people. Still, I felt very isolated, alone, and far from civilization.

There were no roadways, no cars, no railroads, no bridges across streams, no horses, no phones, no local mail service, no electricity, and no radios. The only way to communicate with the outside world was to dispatch couriers. One could not use a bicycle because of swamps and marshes, and the foot trails through the forest were just narrow ruts the width of a bare foot. Pack animals could not live because of the tsetse fly which carried sleeping sickness. Some missionaries had imported horses and donkeys, only to see them die within a few weeks.

While these disadvantages seemed formidable enough, the thing most dreaded by the missionary was the certainty of malaria fever. All of us knew about those who had succumbed to it, and life itself for the rest of us was very uncertain. In the truest sense, one could only hope to live one day at a time.

In his book, *Tropical Africa,* the English explorer Henry Drummond related how he visited the famous Livingstone mission in Nyasaland, only to find the houses, the school, and other buildings spotlessly clean and in order, but not a single missionary present. He wrote:

> Then a native approached and led me a few yards into the forest. And there among the mimosa trees, under a huge granite mountain, were four or five graves. These were the missionaries'.
>
> I spent a day or two in the solemn shadow of that deserted manse. It is one of the loveliest spots in the world. It was hard to believe, sitting under the tamarind trees by the quiet lakeshore, that the pestilence that wasteth at midnight had made this beautiful spot its home.

... Malaria fever is the one sad certainty which every African traveler must face. For months he may escape, but its finger is upon him. And well for him if he has a friend near when it finally overtakes him.[1]

Settling in a New Home

The previous missionaries to Gropaka had not only worked very hard to build as permanent a dwelling as possible, but had brought with them enough woven wire fencing to enclose the mission compound. When we reached the place, most of the wire fence had disappeared. However, we later recognized it in bracelets, anklets, and neck pieces worn by the local inhabitants. Jewelry-wise, the villagers had struck a gold mine! Eventually we managed to replace the fence with posts from a certain tree we found would grow into a hedge if set out just before or during the rainy season before the white ants had time to eat it. The local people called these posts "grow sticks."

After I had finished a room for Blanche, she came over from Blebo and joined me in Gropaka. We were both very anxious to get as much as possible done to finish the work on the place before Ruth arrived. In addition to working on the house, we kept a crew busy clearing the yard which, because of disuse, had grown into a jungle. We held Sunday school and church services under one of the big cottonwood trees for a time.

The old mud and thatch building in the yard which had served as a chapel and school had completely collapsed, so we proceeded to build one to replace it. With a sharp stick I drew a rectangular plan on the ground about thirty by fifty feet, and had the workers dig a small

1. Henry Drummond, *Tropical Africa* (New York: Charles Scribner's Sons, 1891), 41-42.

trench to begin the building operations. Wielding cutlasses, the men cut down small trees in the forest about the size of bean poles, which they drove into the ground about six inches apart. Across these poles we tied split bamboo strips to act as lath to hold mud plaster.

The men dug up tons of dirt at one end of the mission yard, then carried water in jars on their heads from a stream at the foot of the mission hill. With their bare feet they stomped the dirt and water into a thick paste, and smeared it by hand on both sides of the bamboo strips. The walls ended up thicker in some places than others, and they were far from plumb, but they looked good to me and the workers.

Larger trees were cut and carried to the yard for rafters, and gangs of men and boys cut long grass and certain leaves and palm branches for thatch. It was thrilling to watch the long lines of carriers appear in single file, "men as trees walking," with the roofing material on their heads.

When the chapel building was completed we held a dedication service and invited King Jufuli and his elders and the townspeople. The small building was packed African fashion with people sitting on the dirt floor, and there were more people outside than in. Quite a few indicated their desire to repent and serve the Lord, so we were greatly encouraged. At last Gropaka had a chapel where people could hear the gospel message.

During the months I was busy preparing the Gropaka station for Ruth's arrival, she had been dealing with her own challenges of preparing to come to the field. Following is her own account of her call to Africa and how God made a way for her to fulfill it.

Ruth's Report on Preparing for Africa

I was attending an afternoon service in the Newark, New Jersey church of which I was a member, when the pastor called all of us to prayer. According to our custom, each person knelt at his seat and prayed in his own way. While praying I saw, as in a vision, a kind of diagram of an equilateral triangle.

God was the apex at the top, I myself was at the lower left-hand corner, and the continent of Africa was at the lower right-hand corner. I could clearly see a firm line as a connection between God and me, and also a firm line from God to Africa. I took this as an indicator that he loved those people just as much as he loved me. What was missing was a line to connect *me* with Africa. God seemed to speak in my heart saying, *"I love them, but they do not know it. Will you be the connection to go tell them, and complete the triangle?"*

When I told my mother I felt divinely called to go to Africa as a missionary, she strongly resisted the idea. She knew that my experience of receiving the Holy Spirit had radically deepened my commitment to Christ and his Great Commission. But, after all, I was her only daughter, and Africa was a desperately dangerous place. Also, because my parents had divorced, my job as a schoolteacher was an important part of the family's support. So, though I knew God had called me, I felt I couldn't go until Mom was in agreement. All I could do was pray.

Mom also had received the Holy Spirit and was a person of prayer. Often when I returned from work each day I would hear her praying in a back room of the house. I was surprised one day to overhear her praying, "Oh Lord, take care of Ruthie when she goes to Africa and meet all her needs ..." I was thrilled, but wondered what had changed her mind.

"Well," Mom explained when I asked her about it, "the other night

I attended a meeting in which a lady missionary on furlough from India was speaking. She told of standing on the roadside, giving out gospel tracts, when an Indian woman walked by with two small children. One was a healthy-looking toddler, the other a severely crippled youngster in her arms. Hours later when the woman returned along the road, the missionary noticed she no longer had the toddler beside her. Curious, she asked, 'What happened to the little boy you had with you this morning?'

"To her horror the woman replied, 'I sacrificed him to the god of the Ganges.'

"Shocked, the missionary could not help asking, 'But if you had to give up one of your children, why wouldn't you sacrifice the crippled child and keep the healthy one?'

"'Oh, no, you don't understand,' said the woman. 'My god demands my best.'

"So," Mom said to me through her tears, "I cannot keep you back from what God has called you to do. You see, you are my best."

I had accepted Christ when I was eleven years old. After receiving the Holy Spirit when I was a teenager, I firmly decided I would never marry a man unless he was a committed Christian who also had received the Holy Spirit. Then, when I knew I was called to Africa, I determined that any husband for me must also have such a call. Knowing how I felt, some friends predicted I would die an old maid, but for me there was no backing down. God would have to solve the problem.

I met Henry Garlock while he was the roommate of my brother Alfred in Bible school. When we fell in love, and he asked me to be his wife, I found that, lo, all my requirements were met! Convinced that he was the most dedicated young man I had ever known, I promised to join him in Liberia as soon as my teaching contract was fulfilled.

Just to make assurance doubly sure, I visited his family on their farm in Connecticut one weekend. Knowing we were engaged, and wondering whether any woman in the world was good enough for their Henry, the Garlocks decided to test me. After the twelve of us had eaten dinner, they left me alone in the kitchen to see what I would do. When I promptly washed and dried all the dishes, I passed.

I tested them by managing to get the younger children to talk privately about their big brother 'Henny,' as the younger ones called him. When they unanimously poured out impressive stories of his many loving deeds for them, there was no question in my mind about the virtue of this man. He passed with flying colors.

God's provision for my needs as a missionary was just as miraculous as my call, but at first I didn't appreciate his methods. I was accustomed to being independent, providing for myself. One day, as I knelt to pray at the front of our church, a woman came up behind me and put a five-dollar bill in my hand. Frankly, I felt offended. In my prayer I asked, "Lord, do I look so destitute that people think they need to give to me this way?"

"Did I call you to go as a missionary?" he responded.

"Yes, Lord."

"How do you think you'll be supported?"

"Well, Lord, of course I'll depend upon you—after all, you are the one who called me."

"Then don't criticize the way I want to do it," came the answer.

After that, I accepted whatever help people offered without complaint.

In May 1921, I sailed for England on the *S.S. Coronia,* and from there on the *S.S. Patani,* past Spain and Portugal, down the African coast to Cape Palmas.

Ruth's Arrival

On June 25, 1921, a runner arrived at the compound with a cable-gram from Ruth, advising that she had left Liverpool on a freight ship on June 4. I rounded up some hammock men and porters and left Gropaka to go meet her. Reaching Garraway on the coast, I left the hammock men and some of the porters there to wait for Ruth and me to return. I proceeded by surfboat to Cape Palmas, and upon arriving learned that the *Patani* was expected to reach that port early Sunday morning, June 26. I was up at daybreak and saw the ship approaching from a distance.

We had waited so long for this day to come. Eight long months had gone by since Ruth and I had parted in New York. As soon as the ship dropped anchor some distance at sea—it seemed to me to be in the middle of the Atlantic Ocean—I boarded a surfboat with the steamship company's agent and made for the ship. Before leaving shore I had looked through a telescope at the agent's office and seen the *Patani*. There on her deck looking wistfully toward the shore was the most beautiful girl in the whole world—and she was mine! I could hardly wait until we pulled alongside.

It is difficult to describe the thrill of that reunion. We had to wait for the Liberian port officials to go through the formalities of clearing the ship before I was permitted to make my way by a rope ladder up to the deck. At last, at last, we were in each other's arms. Ruth had traveled all those thousands of miles alone, but now the day we had hoped for, prayed for, and dreamed about had finally arrived. We were together in Africa—how good God was to us!

After Ruth had identified her luggage we were put over the side of the ship in a mammy chair and lowered to the surfboat below. It was identical to the experience that Blanche and I had had the previous

December. Steamers called so infrequently at Cape Palmas in those days, and the white people landing there were so few, it was always quite an event for the native oarsmen to be able to row a new missionary ashore. They seemed anxious to show off their rowing skills to Ruth as they took us to the pier.

The Liberian customs officials demanded that everything be unpacked and displayed before them in order to assess duty, so it took considerable time to clear her few belongings. But at last, with arrival formalities complete, we rejoiced that Ruth was on African soil. The wife of the company agent arranged to put her up for the night, and I was able to stay with a European trader. A young Pentecostal brother from Minnesota had boarded the *Patani* in Liverpool and was a fellow passenger of Ruth's all the way to Cape Palmas. He was also headed for an interior mission, so he decided to accompany us as far as Garraway.

The next day, June 27, we engaged a surfboat for Garraway. Our experience was similar to the one described earlier, although having a stronger wind for the sail, we reached Garraway in a shorter period of time. But riding in the open surfboat from Cape Palmas was very trying. Some have managed to escape seasickness all the way from New York to the Cape, and then become desperately ill on the small surfboat. Both Ruth and the other new missionary were very seasick. We reached Garraway rather late in the evening.

Ruth wrote the following report of her arrival there:

When we reached Garraway it was pitch black and I could see absolutely nothing. The boatmen were all talking at once and shouting at someone on shore. The bow of the surfboat ran onto the sandy beach and stopped. Then there was a mad scramble and I was totally in the dark in more ways than one.

"Honey, just sit still where you are until someone comes for you," Henry called out. So I sat. A short time later I heard a black man say, "Mammy, you ready go now?" I said, "Yes, I'm ready," and stood up.

He took my arm and led me very carefully to the prow and said, "Now stand still." I could not see him or anything else, but heard him moving around. He had stepped over the side into the water which was about knee deep for him. Then he said, "Mammy, come." I put my arm out to grope for something to hold onto to steady me, and found his outstretched arm. Then I asked, "How am I ever going to get to shore through the water?"

"Mammy, I go carry you," he answered. So saying, he picked me up as one would a small child, one strong arm under my shoulders and one under my knees. He carried me through the surf and stood me on a rock and said, "Don't move." Henry had been carried ashore piggyback and had sent this oarsman back to carry me.

In a few seconds Henry spoke: "Don't be afraid, Honey. It's so awfully dark, but you're all right now." Then he led me along the sandy beach to the mission house, whose lighted windows were a welcome sight.

Our Wedding

While waiting for Edgar Personeus to arrive at Garraway to perform the marriage ceremony, Ruth and I packed her outfit in headload-size bundles for the porters. We tried to make them waterproof, but this was not always possible. We usually did tie banana leaves around most of the bundles.

We were married at three o'clock in the afternoon, June 28, 1921. Mr. and Mrs. Howard (who had arrived in Liberia with Blanche and me) stood up with us, and the audience was made up of our hammock men and porters. I had secured a marriage license from a British colonial official in Cape Palmas a few days before. Ruth had given me her class ring from normal school (a teacher's college) before we parted in New York. Using this as a model for size, I had hired a native blacksmith in Cape Palmas to make a wedding ring for me to give her, using the gold from an English sovereign coin. With another gold sovereign I paid him for making the ring. Ruth was always very proud of her African-made wedding ring.

The day after the wedding we arose at two o'clock in the morning and started for Newaka. For the first leg of the journey, Ruth and I each rode in a small dugout canoe on a crocodile-infested river. It was several miles to the landing where our hammock men were to meet us for the trek through the jungle. It was almost pitch black with no moon, but the African oarsmen seemed able to find their way around bends in the stream and under the overhanging branches of the swampland. I warned Ruth to keep her hands inside her canoe because of the crocodiles.

After we disembarked from the canoes, Ruth was carried by hammock over the bush trail. But because it had been difficult to get hammock men, I walked all the way to Newaka. It was a long, hard trip, as we had not taken sufficient time to rest at Garraway after the ordeal in the surfboat coming from Cape Palmas. But because the rainy season had begun, I felt compelled to press on before the streams and marshes became completely impassable.

Beaten by the rain, it was very difficult for the carriers to walk the slippery, snakelike trail. At times we had to wade in water waist-deep. Mile after mile we sloshed along. As David Livingstone once said about a trip with his family in the rain, "We got soaked by going on, and sodden if we stood still."

Finally we reached Newaka mission station just before dark, seemingly more dead than alive. I had been able to secure only four hammock men for Ruth for the trip, which under the circumstances was really not sufficient. The four alternated in carrying the hammock, but from slipping and sliding in the mud, and wading swamps and streams, these fine African men were taxed almost to the limit of their strength. In fact, one of the men called Banker (a name given him earlier by a sea captain), drenched again and again on the trip, contracted malaria soon afterward and died two or three days after reaching his home in Gropaka. He was one of the most courteous and kindhearted men, and was very solicitous of Ruth's well-being because she was a new missionary. He frequently would ask in his Pidgin English, "How we go do for Mammy?"

The missionaries at Newaka wanted us to stay over for a few days. But because of threatening rain, and knowing that Blanche was waiting for us at Gropaka, we wanted to reach our journey's end as soon as possible. So we kept trekking, and arrived in Gropaka at 3:00 P.M. on June 30, 1921. Blanche and the school children and many of the townspeople were gathered to greet us. What a great welcome they gave to Ruth and me—it was a dream come true that we were together at our own home in Africa. But we were several days recuperating from the effects of the long, hard trip from Cape Palmas.

King Jufuli of Gropaka presented us with a young steer to butcher in celebration of our wedding, and blind Moses Ty gave us a goat. We supplied a hundred pounds of rice and our mission boys cut several bunches of palm nuts from palm trees surrounding the compound to cook with the meat as gravy or sauce—known to the people as palm butter—which was in turn strongly seasoned with red pepper. It took several hours to prepare the meal, but only a few minutes for the crowd that gathered to devour every bit of it.

After the wedding feast we conducted a gospel service in which many indicated a desire to follow Christ. Delighted to be doing what we had come so many miles to do, we looked forward to ministering to the people of Gropaka in the days ahead.

FOUR

MIRACLE AT THE SORRIKA RIVER

I was no prophet, neither was I a prophet's son; but I was an herd-man, and a gatherer of sycamore fruit: And the Lord took me as I followed the flock, And the Lord said unto me, "Go ..."

AMOS 7:14-15

About a week after Ruth and I arrived at Gropaka, a runner came with a letter from the mission station at Newaka saying Esther Sandstrom was very ill with malaria. The other two lady missionaries there said they were both nearly worn out from caring for the sick, and suggested that perhaps Blanche would be willing to come to Newaka to help with the nursing. She hated to leave Gropaka so soon after Ruth's arrival, but felt duty-bound to respond to the appeal. So she left early the next day with a few carriers and managed to get across the Sorrika River before it overflowed its banks.

About midnight four days later, runners brought the sad news of Esther's death and a request from the Newaka missionaries that I come there to conduct the funeral service. They also wrote that Blanche had come down with malaria upon her arrival at Newaka and was running a high fever.

Remember, it was an unwritten rule of the mission that no new missionary be left alone until after having had his or her first attack of malaria. Ruth hadn't had her first fever yet, and it was risky to leave her alone. But we both felt there was no choice but for me to hurry to

Newaka to bury Esther and see what could be done for Blanche. I immediately sent a runner to Nynabo to ask Sophia Nygaard, one of the missionaries there, to come and stay with Ruth while I was gone. Promising to return just as soon as possible, I left early on July 12 for Newaka. Sophia arrived at Gropaka shortly after I left.

Crossing the River

The letter carriers who had come the night before told us they had experienced great difficulty in reaching us at Gropaka because the river was beginning to flood. As I approached the Sorrika River I wondered whether it would be possible for me to get to Newaka without serious difficulty. Under normal circumstances I would not have attempted to cross the river at that time of year. But knowing the brokenhearted missionaries were expecting me to help comfort them and conduct Esther's funeral, I prayed that God would go before me.

As I came closer to the stream I saw that not only was the river a raging torrent, but the lowlands on either side of the river were flooded as well. What was I to do? I stood on a piece of high ground looking out across the flooded area and the swirling stream beyond, wondering just how I could get to the other side. That is all I remember.

The next thing I knew, I was walking into the yard of the Newaka mission station. My clothes were not wet, except from perspiration, and none of my carriers were with me. They did not reach Newaka until many hours later. Ruth later told me that some of my porters had returned to Gropaka that same day saying they could not get across the Sorrika, and they did not know what had happened to me. They had never caught up with me. This of course caused Ruth great concern, but she knew she had no recourse except to ask for God's protection for me.

Wedding Bells for Henry and Ruth,
June 28, 1921, at Garraway, Liberia.

Henry and Ruth revisit Garraway
January 29, 1946.

Henry Garlock
1920

Ruth E. Trotter
1920

The mission house in Gropaka, the Garlocks' first home in Liberia in 1921.

The Garlock's home in Rhodilly, Pahn, 1922.

H. B. Garlock standing on huge anthill created by white ants, at Gropaka miss-
sion station in 1921. His sister, Blanche is standing at right.

MR. and MRS. H. B. GARLOCK

John and Ruth

FOREIGN ADDRESS

Tamale, Northern Territories
Gold Coast, West Africa

HOME ADDRESS

1139 So. Market St.,   Wichita, Kansas

Copy of the prayer card circulated by the Garlocks in 1931 when they were
preparing to go to Northern Ghana. They sailed in January, 1932.

Mission Bungalow in Tamale, (pronounced Tah'-mah-lee), Northern Ghana.
Built by the Garlocks in 1932-1933.

H. B. Garlock in 1933 in front of the church he built in Tamale, Ghana.
The church remains today.

« On earth peace, good will toward men »
LUKE 2: 14

With all good wishes for a delightful
Christmas and a happy New Year

MR. AND MRS. H. B. GARLOCK
JOHN AND RUTH

ASSEMBLIES OF GOD MISSION
TAMALE

A Christmas card sent by the Garlocks from Tamale, Northern Ghana,
in December 1934.

H. B. Garlock preaching near Yendi, Northern Ghana. Ruth Garlock playing a portable pump organ. John and Ruthie sitting behind their father. Circa 1932.

Ruth Suehn (the Garlocks' African daughter) with her husband Benjamin, a Methodist pastor, and three of their children. The boy on the left was named Henry after H. B. Garlock. Date of photo unknown, circa 1940s.

Henry in 1940, when he and Ruth were pastors of Full Gospel Tabernacle at Seventh and Riverview, Kansas City, Kansas.

Ruth Garlock in 1940, when she and Henry were pastors of Full Gospel
Tabernacle at Seventh and Riverview, Kansas City, Kansas.

Ruth Suehn and "Ma" Garlock, as she was affectionately know, in Barclayville, January 30, 1946.

The grave of Reverend Gortner, father of J. Narver Gortner, who died in 1888. H. B. Garlock visited the grave in Garraway, Liberia in 1946.

On a visit to Liberia in 1946, H. B. Garlock sometimes used the traditional form of travel by hammock carriers.

June 1951.

H. B. Garlock
1947

Ruth and Henry Garlock in Switzerland to celebrate their
50th wedding anniversary. June 1971.

The Garlocks in San José, California after they retired. August 13, 1977.

Ruth Garlock on her last missions trip with one of the children at the Christian Haitian Outreach Orphanage in 1986. She was 89 years old.

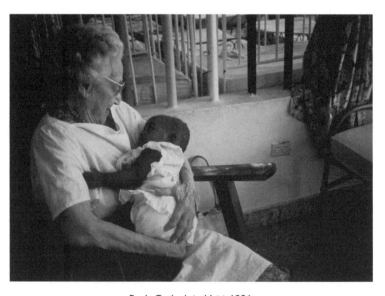

Ruth Garlock in Haiti, 1986.

In the midst of their sorrow the missionaries at Newaka asked me how I got across the Sorrika waters. I simply told them that the Lord had helped me—I didn't know what else to say. Whether I was carried by the Spirit, as Philip was transported to Azotus (see Acts 8:39-40), I do not know. But I do know that all things are possible with God. The miracle was not performed for my sake, but for the sake of the grief-stricken missionaries who needed help at the time. I could never give any other explanation but that it was a miracle of God.

Esther Sandstrom was laid to rest beside a number of other missionary heroes who "loved not their lives unto the death" (Revelation 12:11), and of whom the world was not worthy. She was a zealous and dedicated Swedish sister, and greatly loved by all who knew her.

Blanche was still bedfast and unable to attend the funeral. But the next day she begged me to take her home with me to Gropaka, claiming she could smell death everywhere in the mission house. "They will call you to bury me in a few days if you do not take me home with you," she said.

The other missionaries advised her to wait until she was stronger before attempting the trip to Gropaka. But I knew that if she did die at Newaka within the next few days, I would never forgive myself for abandoning her. Her plea was that Gropaka was her home, and Ruth would be glad to help care for her until she was strong again. Under such circumstances, what else could I do except grant her request?

While I was still at Newaka, word came from Blebo that Mrs. Personeus, who also was suffering from malaria, had nearly died the day before. It seemed the very air was laden with death. And so, against the warnings and seemingly good advice of the other missionaries, I decided to take Blanche with me and trust God with the outcome. I confess I was moved by her tears and the thought of her dying away from Ruth and me. She was only twenty-one years old.

Our Return Journey

I hired some hammock men to carry Blanche, as she was too weak to walk, and we started out early the next morning for Gropaka. Remembering how the Lord had helped me on my way to the funeral, I hoped that we might enjoy a similar experience on our way home. However, this was not to be. Long before reaching the main Sorrika stream we found the lowlands flooded as high as waist deep. I had the porters cut down trees and tried to make a raft with green logs, but it soon sank under my weight. I told Blanche that she had better let me return her to Newaka, and I would come for her at a later date. But she insisted that if I left her I would never see her alive again. So we struggled on.

By having Blanche carried on the shoulders and heads of the hammock men, we finally reached the brink of the main channel. After what seemed like hours of maneuvering, some of the husky carriers succeeded in stretching long "tie-tie" vines across the raging torrent and tied them to large trees on either side of the river. This they did by plunging into the swift current far above the place of the proposed crossing and being carried downstream as they fought their way to the opposite bank. After the men secured the vines and assured us that they would hold our weight, we pushed out into the main current, holding the vine rope to steady us.

Bestman, a strong Christian from Gropaka, took the lead. Blanche, who could not swim, and was so ill with malaria, followed. We placed the vine rope under her armpits and I followed close behind, trying to hold her up. Although the vine rope bowed downstream with our weight, we got along fairly well until we reached the middle of the stream and started to pull ourselves up on the other side. Then we were knocked off balance, our feet carried straight out downstream by the force of the current.

Halfway across, Blanche completely collapsed and became like a dead weight. When the current pulled her under several times in spite of our efforts to keep her head above water, it seemed she would drown in spite of all we could do. But big, strong Bestman said, "Suppose Mammy go die today? Me too—I go die with her." And he meant it.

Just when it seemed we could go no farther, or that the vine would certainly break, we managed to pull ourselves along hand over hand, a few inches at a time, until we finally reached the opposite bank. If Bestman and I had not been given supernatural strength, I know we never could have made it. And we still had to wade through waist-deep water for about a quarter of a mile.

There was no place where we could change our wet clothes, and no dry ones to be had in any case. So we struggled on to Gropaka until we reached our own mission compound in the middle of the night.

How relieved Ruth was that I had survived the journey. As a young bride of less than two weeks, she had already come face to face with the possibility of being left a widow. Blanche was several days recovering from the ordeal, but she was thrilled to be back home in Gropaka again with Ruth and me.

The Fever Strikes

Some historians have estimated that during the decade or two after Livingstone and Stanley, as many as one-third of the pioneer missionaries throughout Africa died within a year of reaching the field. Most of them, in their early twenties, never survived their first attack of malaria. Had they lived, their names might have been listed among Africa's great. No doubt, for some, loneliness and homesickness played a big part in hastening their deaths.

Just six weeks after reaching the field, Ruth came down with her first attack of malaria. She had gotten up that morning, as she said, "feeling funny." She sat at the sewing machine for about two hours, making clothes for the school children. At the lunch table she said she felt cold and asked Matthew, our houseboy, to bring her a sweater. When I served her plate she looked at it, then at me and said, shivering, "I just can't eat." It dawned on me she was coming down with malaria, so I sent her to bed. When she called for me a little later, I went into the bedroom and found her having such violent chills the bed was shaking. We piled all available blankets on her until she said she couldn't move.

After awhile the chills subsided; then the fever came. And off came the layers of blankets. About ten o'clock that night her fever broke, leaving her perspiring profusely and feeling so weak she thought she would be an invalid for the rest of her life. But very gradually her strength returned. For her twenty-fourth birthday on August 12 I made a cake—after sifting the bugs and worms from the moldy flour. She was able to come to the table for a little while, and in two days' time was completely recovered.

Speaking of baking cakes, I remember one occasion when a small keg of flour we had ordered from Cape Palmas arrived at our station very dark, moldy, and filled with bugs and worms. With my next order of supplies, I sent a letter by carrier to the manager of the trading post, describing the poor condition of this particular batch of flour. (None of the flour we purchased was ever good, but this batch was worse than most.) A short time later I received a letter from him as follows:

Cavalla River Trading Company
Cape Palmas
15 September 1921

H.B. Garlock, Esquire
Gropaka Station
Interior

Dear Mr. Garlock:

I have this morning received your favor of the 5th instant, and much regret to note that the flour recently purchased from us was received in such a bad condition. I have consulted my private information bureau and learned that the barrel was accidently dropped in the water during the unloading operation at Garraway. This will account for the sepia tint.

The animal life in the barrel is of course inevitable in West Africa, and after a time one gets used to bugs instead of currants. This is a live firm, and all our flour is live stuff! So I refrain from inflicting another barrel of horrors on you. Instead, I am sending you by bearer 36 yards of blue baft [a thin, blue material used for trading] and trust you will find this in order.

Regarding the previous barrel, I think the best thing you can do about it is bury it. If you don't want to have it under your particular compound, just direct it to Cape Palmas. It will no doubt come home itself.

Yours sincerely,
William S. Murdoch

The original letter from Mr. Murdoch was framed under glass and long displayed in the foyer of the Gospel Publishing House in Springfield, Missouri. Perhaps, without a sense of humor, none of us would have survived in West Africa in those days.

FIVE

CHALLENGING FETISH WORSHIP

And these signs will follow those who believe: In my name they will cast out demons; they will speak with new tongues;... they will lay hands on the sick, and they will recover.

MARK 16:17-18

The main entrance to Gropaka village was guarded by a large fetish or "juju house" which the local people provided to house and appease their ancestral spirits. All who entered the village had to pass under it. The structure was built in the form of an arch made of wooden poles and thatched with grass, and on either side of the arch was a settee made of bamboo poles.

Sitting on one of the settees was an image of a man made with mud, shells, and goat's hair. On the opposite side were two earthen jars, which served as beehives. The bees were a part of the fetish and were considered sacred, but they could be menacing at times to people passing through the arch going to or from the village. Our mission station was located on a hill at the opposite side of town from the big juju.

We had noticed that many of the people wore fetishes around their necks or about their waists, and fetish charms hung from above the doorways of their huts. The local fetish priest or witch doctor often directed special celebrations in honor of the village fetish. On moonlit nights the people would sometimes sing and dance all night long, accompanied by the beating of drums. Like most primitive African tribes, the Barroba people were very superstitious. By wearing fetishes on their bodies they believed they could be protected from wild animals and hostile tribes. They thought the fetishes guaranteed that no sickness could overtake them, and that they would be assured of long life. Parents or grandparents often hung fetishes around the necks of babies and little children.

The local people also believed that certain fetishes assured them of a good crop of rice with a minimum amount of work. And other more expensive fetishes could be bought from the witch doctor, which supposedly would enable them to have large families. Like the silversmiths of Ephesus (see Acts 19:24-25), the fetish priests of West Africa depended on the superstition of the people for their livelihood.

Our hearts were stirred when we saw the people of Gropaka given over almost entirely to this demonic fetish worship. Surely we had come to the right place to preach the gospel! Each day we conducted a morning service at the mission, followed by three hours of school for the forty to fifty boys and girls who had come to live on the compound. In those days it was customary to provide room and board for the children attending the mission school.

Each evening, whenever possible, we conducted services in the middle of the town with the help of our interpreter, Ernest Weah, a pastor who had served under other missionaries. We found that some of the local people could understand Pidgin English, which we picked up from our fellow workers. Later we acquired some of the Barroba language.

In our preaching we frequently assured our listeners that Christ could deliver them from the fear of evil spirits and give them genuine peace in their hearts, which they never experienced through fetish worship. Being very zealous for the Lord, we wanted to see the people renounce their heathen ways and accept Christ at once. But our zeal was not always tempered with knowledge.

One evening while preaching in the village I pointed out to King Jufuli and his elders that it certainly did not look right for them to have a heathen fetish shrine at one entrance to their village and a Christian mission station at the other. Previously we had related the accounts of Jesus cleansing the lepers, opening the eyes of the blind, and even raising the dead. On this occasion I proceeded to preach about Elijah challenging the priests of Baal on Mount Carmel. I quoted Elijah's words, "How long halt ye between two opinions? If the Lord be God, follow him: but if Baal, then follow him" (1 Kings 18:21, KJV).

I told them how the priests of Baal appealed to their god to send fire and consume the sacrifices they had placed on their altar—but saw no results. Elijah placed a sacrifice on the altar which he had built, and he even had the people pour water over it three times. When the prophet prayed, God sent down fire from heaven and consumed Elijah's sacrifice. The people responded by proclaiming, "The Lord, he is God!" (v. 39).

Two missionaries had laid down their lives in Gropaka while pioneering the gospel among these primitive people. And now we were trying to build on their foundation. Surely it was now time to press the leaders for a decision. Or was it?

"Show Us God's Power ..."

When I had finished speaking, I asked the chief and his elders to give us their answer. Were they ready to renounce their fetish worship and follow the God who answers by fire and the Christ that we preached? Or should we consider going to another tribe with the gospel?

My challenge was premature. As long as I live I shall never forget the chief's reply. This is the essence of what he said:

White man, you have asked us to give up the religion of our ancestors for a new religion, one that has not been tried by our people. You tell us that your God has all power—that he can cleanse the leper, open the eyes of the blind, and raise the dead. You have just told us about Elijah's God sending down fire from heaven. But we have not yet seen any fire nor any power of the God you talk about. Our fetish priests have performed miracles for many years, or so we believe. Our fathers died trusting in the power of fetishes, as did their fathers before them.

We are prepared to consider serving your God, but before doing so we would like to see a demonstration of this power you talk about. There are many lepers in our village—would you mind healing some of them? (The chief and two of his elders had leprosy.) There are many blind among us. Please heal some of these. And our people are dying every day.

While the chief was speaking, his words were interrupted by the piercing wail of a mother whose baby had died in her arms. The other pagan women soon gathered at her hut and sympathetically began to wail with her. After all these years we have sometimes awakened in the night and imagined we could hear that hopeless, helpless, Christless wail of the lost which we heard so many times in those early years in Africa.

With that woeful sound in the background, the chief ended with his own challenge to us:

As soon as we witness some of the miracles you have preached about take place among our people, we will seriously consider destroying the big fetish as you suggest.

So instead of putting King Jufuli and the people of Gropaka on the spot, we ourselves were now on the spot. How could we answer this chief? What could we tell the people? I had to admit that everything King Jufuli had said was logical. It was now time for us to practice what we preached.

We returned home that night wondering whether we should just pack up and leave the country. I vowed I would never preach in the village again until God did something for us. For days we prayed and lay on our faces before the Lord, reminding him of his promise in Mark 16:17: "These signs shall follow them that believe...."

We said, "Lord, if these signs are not to follow the missionaries who have obeyed your command to go to all the world, then who are they to follow?" We fasted and prayed and asked the school children living on the compound to join us in fasting and prayer one day a week for an outpouring of the Holy Spirit. As a result of getting them to seek the Lord, many of these boys and girls definitely were saved, and some of them received the baptism in the Holy Spirit.

We Begin to See Miracles

King Jufuli had sent one of his sons to the mission school. James was about twelve or fourteen, and was almost blind from cataracts on his eyes. One morning in devotions when I read the story of how Jesus had healed blind Bartimaeus (see Mark 10), James came forward for prayer and asked, "Do you think Jesus is able to heal my eyes?"

After what had taken place in town a few weeks before, I knew this was no time to hedge or beat about the bush. Taking a bold step of faith, I told him that if he would completely surrender his life to God to do his will, that Jesus would heal him just as he had done for blind Bartimaeus.

James knelt down and cried out to God with all his might—I suppose much as blind Bartimaeus had done at Jericho. When I knew James really meant business, I knelt down beside him and laid my hands upon his eyes. I asked God, for Jesus' sake, for the sake of James' heathen father, and for the sake of the people of Gropaka who had asked to see a miracle of God's power, to please heal this boy.

Suddenly James opened his eyes and looked up. I could see that the cataracts had completely disappeared—his eyes were clear. His face lit up, and without saying a word he jumped to his feet, dashed out the door of the chapel, and ran all the way to town to his father's house to show him what God had done. The murky film that had covered his eyes was gone, and the boy could see. Because he was the son of the chief, news of his healing soon spread throughout the entire town of Gropaka.

Saved From the Dung Heap

The leading hammock carrier in town—a strong, muscular man named Gredeji—had a wife who became very ill. She had not properly recovered after giving birth to her last child, and she steadily grew weaker. Besides this problem, she also had leprosy. During our visits to town we repeatedly had called at the Gredeji hut to see this poor, emaciated, dying woman. Then one day, not long after James' eyes were healed, we heard the familiar death wail—a sound which carried all the way out to our compound when the wind was right. One of the school children in our yard, understanding the meaning of the sound, told us that Gredeji's wife had died.

Instead of burying their dead, the people of Gropaka carried the corpses to a fetish grove on a little hilltop not far from town. There the bodies were left for the hyenas, jackals, and vultures to devour. When the wind came from that direction the odor of decaying human flesh was almost unbearable. (After some months we persuaded the chief and his elders to override the wishes of the fetish priests and break with their fathers' heathen custom and bury their dead. When they finally agreed to this, we felt it was quite an achievement.)

But now, the body of Gredeji's poor wife was destined for the grove. Late in the afternoon, as was our custom, we walked into Gropaka where the people, especially the children, always gathered around us. We decided to stop at Gredeji's hut to offer our condolences for his bereavement.

A large group of people, mostly women, had gathered outside the hut and were weeping and wailing. We were appalled to see the woman's naked body lying on a refuse heap nearby. She had wasted away to mere skin and bone, and in the days before her death she looked like a skeleton. But as we looked at the body about to be taken to the fetish grove where all the dead were placed, I noticed a slight twitching of her muscles.

I said to Gredeji, "You're not going to the grove yet, are you? I just saw a slight movement in her body."

He said, "That doesn't mean anything; that will stop before we get to the grove."

We could detect no heartbeat or other sign of life, and it seemed to us from the foul odor that decomposition had already set in. As I looked at the corpse on the refuse heap and heard and saw the weeping people around it, I suddenly felt God spoke to my heart. *"This is the opportunity you've been waiting for,"* I heard him say. *"The people have been asking for a demonstration of the power of God. You pray for this woman and I'll raise her up."*

But my reasoning said, "Oh no, Lord, this is an impossible case! Let me pray for a person with some minor ailment." Then I realized that I couldn't heal anything, not even a mosquito bite. A God who can perform one miracle can perform all miracles, even to the raising of the dead.

Turning to Ruth, I said, "I believe God has told me that if I will pray for this woman, he will raise her up."

I was afraid she would think I had lost my mind, but I was under-estimating the faith of the mate God had given me. "If you feel this is the will of God, go ahead and pray for her and I'll stand in agreement with you," she said confidently.

So before Gredeji could begin the procession to the fetish grove with his wife's body, I asked him, "Are you satisfied that no fetish med-icine or any other power on earth can raise this woman up?"

"Of course—there is no medicine strong enough to raise the dead!" he replied.

I was so sure that God had spoken to me that I sent for King Jufuli and some of his elders. When they came I asked them the same ques-tion I had asked Gredeji. They gave the same reply.

Then I announced loudly for all to hear, "We are going to pray and ask God to raise this woman up and heal her, for his glory."

Ruth and I knelt beside the body on the dung heap and began to pray aloud. I reminded the Lord we had come to Africa at his com-mand, and told him that the heathen king of these people had asked for a demonstration of God's power, which we felt was only reason-able. Then I asked him to touch this woman with his healing power. As I concluded, the quiet prayer under my breath was, "Dear Lord, your cause is at stake."

After I had prayed, Ruth and I laid hands on the corpse and rebuked death and the devil in the name of the Lord Jesus Christ. Instantly the body began to shake violently up and down on the ground. The woman's body was lifted up as though it were levitating, so we could see between the corpse and the trash heap under it. Terrified, the people scattered in every direction.

Then, to the amazement of everybody, the shaking ceased, and the woman sat up and asked for food.

We called on the people to praise God for this mighty manifestation of his power in raising this woman from the dead. When I told Gredeji to kill a chicken and have the women prepare a meal for his wife, they immediately followed my instructions.

A short while later, as we were leaving Gropaka village for home, a runner met us on the path. He delivered a letter from a lady missionary in Nynabo requesting that I come there at once, as her coworker was dying of malaria fever and she wanted me to be on hand to bury her. The letter said that Miss Eustace had already laid out the dress she wanted to be buried in, and had given instructions to send certain keepsakes home to her mother in Virginia.

I took a kerosene lantern and a few mission boys and walked all night to reach the Nynabo station. But this time I did not conduct a funeral. The raising of Gredeji's wife had greatly strengthened my faith to trust God for healing. After much prayer, and my encouraging her to roll her burden on the Lord, Miss Eustace was soon able to be up and about. She served three or four more mission terms after that. Some twenty-five years later I visited her grave under a palm tree in Pahn territory.

On my way back to Gropaka from Nynabo I was myself smitten with a severe case of malaria fever and sun fever. But I trusted God to raise me up just as he had raised up those for whom I'd recently prayed. After several days in bed, I began regaining my strength.

The Miracle Confirmed

As soon as I was able to walk again, Ruth and I resumed our regular schedule of going into Gropaka village just before sunset. One of the first places we visited was the home of hammock-carrier Gredeji. When he appeared I immediately asked him about his wife's health. He smiled and said she was perfectly well and would soon be coming in from the rice farm where she had been working that day. I could hardly believe my ears.

I said, "Look, Gredeji, you're a heathen man and probably have a number of wives, as is the custom of your people. But I am speaking of the woman whose remains you were about to take to the fetish grove about three weeks ago ... the woman we prayed for. Where is she?"

"Master, that's the woman I'm talking about," he replied. "Your God raised her from the dead, and here she comes now."

We looked up, and here came a woman with a huge load of firewood on her head. On top of the wood was a large stalk of bananas—a tremendous burden for any woman to carry. When she had lowered the heavy load to the ground, I asked her her name. She gave us the name of the woman the townspeople were wailing over a few weeks before. I asked her who had made her well. Her face lit up and she pointed to the sky and said, *"Nyisoa,"* meaning God.

Having myself just been healed of a terrible dose of sun fever, and still rather shaky, I suppose I got a little excited. But I was so thrilled that I went to the center of town and began beating the large "palaver drum." The people poured into town from every direction to find out what the palaver was all about. When they had gathered I stood before them with the woman who had been raised from the dead, and asked whether they knew this woman. They admitted that they did.

"Who is it that has restored this woman to life?" I asked.

Of course the voices cried out, *"Nyisoa, Nyisoa!"*

Taking advantage of their response I said, "Let us all give thanks to God for performing this miracle, proving that he has more power than all the fetishes in the world." So we had a great praise service right there in the middle of the heathen village.

King Jufuli renounced fetish worship and accepted the Lord, as did most of the members of his council. He witnessed throughout his realm of how God had blessed the people of Gropaka after they gave up fetish worship and accepted Christ. Jufuli's son, James, received the Holy Spirit and continued his education at the Gropaka mission school.

As for Gredeji, he took a strong stand for the Lord after his wife was raised from the dead, and witnessed to everyone in the Barroba region of what God had done.

SIX

BURNING OF THE BIG FETISH

Let us have grace, by which we may serve God acceptably with
reverence and godly fear: For our God is a consuming fire.
HEBREWS 12:28b-29

It quickly became apparent that God's response to our prayer for Gredeji's wife to be restored to life had a far-reaching impact.

The very next morning following our praise service in Gropaka, King Jufuli and his elders paid a visit to the mission. Receiving the delegation into our home, we observed the important custom of serving tea. Protocol required that we offer such hospitality to guests before bringing up any serious topics of discussion.

After tea, the chief told us that he and his council of elders had discussed the recent miracle they had seen with their own eyes, and they were now convinced they no longer needed the fetish shrine. "The God you serve is more powerful than our fetishes, and able to protect us from all evil," he said.

Then he suggested that perhaps I would like to destroy the fetish at my convenience—explaining that they themselves could not destroy it for fear of reprisals from the fetish priests. Although they were giving their permission for us to remove the shrine, the elders preferred that we not do it immediately, as they did not want the witch doctors to suspect them of having asked us to do this. In due respect for the chief's request, I didn't act right away.

But after waiting for a few days, we took a group of our mission boys and made our way to the big fetish. Using a bundle of split bamboo as a torch, we set fire to the shrine that had guarded the entrance to the village for so many years. As the structure began to burn, many of the Gropaka townspeople gathered around. Some of the older ones called King Jufuli to the scene and told him to stop us, for they feared that great calamity would come to the village if the fetish were destroyed.

"If the fetish has any power at all, it can defend itself," the chief told them firmly.

This reminded us of the Old Testament account of Gideon pulling down the altar of Baal and offering up a bullock to the Lord in its place. When told of the deed, Gideon's father said, "If he [Baal] is a god, let him plead for himself, because his altar has been torn down!" (Judges 6:31).

"Honey in the Rock"

Of course the "god" made with human hands could not defend itself, so it soon burned to the ground. Only the two beehive jars, filled with honey, were left. After most of the bees had escaped, our mission boys picked up the jars and began eating honey from them. Alarmed at their boldness, some of the villagers told the boys that they would surely die, because the honey was part of the fetish altar.

"This honey now belongs to the Lord," they declared. "We're not afraid of harm coming to us, or to the village." Then they began singing an old gospel song we had taught them—"Oh, taste and see that the Lord is good; it tastes like honey in the rock!"

Since the destruction of the fetish had drawn a crowd of witnesses, we took the opportunity to conduct a gospel service while we were in town. Some of our Christians gave testimony of what the Lord had done for them, including James, the king's son who had been healed of blindness. We emphasized the great love of God who sent his son, Jesus, to set them free—contrasting his love and mercy with the religion of fear that had caused them to rely on fetishes for protection. Then I asked how many wanted to discard their fetishes and follow the Lord.

Many of them removed the charms from their bodies and brought the idols and jujus from their homes, throwing them in a heap in the middle of the circle. We set fire to these objects and had a great time of rejoicing and praising God. It was like a replay of Paul's experience at Ephesus as recorded in Acts 19:18-19: "And many that believed came, and confessed, and showed their deeds. Many of them also which used curious arts brought their books together, and burned them before all men."

As a result of these miracles—the healing of the blind boy and the raising of the dead woman—there was a great outpouring of the Holy Spirit. And not only upon the people of Gropaka. The revival spread throughout much of the Barroba territory. After burning their fetishes and idols, the people in that area prospered as never before. This was one of the greatest moves of God Ruth and I ever witnessed, either in Africa or in the United States.

On one occasion a few months later, I overheard King Jufuli talking with the chief of another large village about fetish worship. Apparently the other chief still trusted in his fetishes for protection. Jufuli told him that since the people of Gropaka had given up fetish worship and accepted the missionary's God, the Lord Jesus Christ, they were happier and more prosperous than they had ever been before.

Understanding Atonement for Sin

Some ten years later, when we were working in another part of Africa, my wife had an experience that illustrates how an inborn impulse to try to atone for sins seems to be a universal trait. Ruth noticed that one of our workers, Boomwah, would leave his duties from time to time to go with other men of the tribe to a grove just beyond our compound for a special ceremony. She asked one day if she could go with him, and he agreed. She followed him into the grove, then stood to one side and watched as the shaman, using a flat rock for an altar, slit the neck of a chicken. Spilling some of the blood on the rock, he then dabbed a bit of blood on the forehead of each man present.

"Why do your people do this, Boomwah?" she asked after they had returned to the mission house.

"To take away our sins," he answered.

"Do you believe it really does?"

"We hope so, white woman, we hope so," he replied as his gaze held hers. Then shaking his head as his voice trailed away, he said forlornly, "But who can know?"

No matter how many sacrifices one offers, or how many rituals one performs, does that change the heart of the worshiper? Or assuage his guilt? Boomwah's question echoes through every culture: *Who can know?*

Because he had a fairly good grasp of English, Boomwah often served as an interpreter for us and the other missionaries on our preaching trips. This repeated exposure to the gospel caused him to come to faith himself before very long and to be assured that Jesus made a way for his sins to be forgiven.

Blanche Returns to the U.S.

Though Blanche had at first seemed to recover from her earlier attack of malaria, it was not long before she began to suffer with repeated bouts of fever. They grew worse and worse as the weeks went by. At times she would become quite delirious from running such a high temperature. Finally, Ruth and I felt we must send her home in order to save her life, with the hope that she could return after regaining her health.

We knew of many others who had been compelled to leave Africa after a few months. Our mentor, William Johnson, contracted malaria during his first term and had to leave after only seven months on the field. But he regained his health and later was able to return to Liberia and experience many years of successful ministry.

So after seeing Blanche suffer much and grow weaker and weaker, we sent her home with Sophia Nygaard who was returning to Canada for a well-earned furlough. I escorted the two women to the coast and saw them safely on board a ship for England in February 1922. After recuperating for a time there, Blanche was able to continue her journey home to America. She later married Ruth's brother, Alfred Trotter, and they came to Liberia together.

Another Miracle

African Christians, like believers anywhere in the world, have their severe tests from time to time. Tragically, some of them fall by the way. But having once cut loose from pagan customs and taken a stand for Christ, an African generally is not fully accepted back into pagan society even if he does choose to return to his old ways. A backslidden

African Christian is indeed an outcast from both the pagan society and the Christian fellowship. His only recourse is to go off by himself and establish a home in a new location, usually some distance from both his native town and the mission station.

Philip, who had become a Christian through the influence of workers at another mission, was one of these unfortunates. One day he came to our station at Gropaka while I was away on trek and introduced himself to Ruth. She describes what happened:

Philip confessed his backsliding and asked if he could please bring his dying wife to the station, so that when she died she could be buried in the mission cemetery. Of course I said yes. I offered him my hammock so she could be brought in with some degree of primitive comfort. He thanked me, took the hammock, and left.

One afternoon a few days later I heard a commotion in the yard, and there was Philip with quite a crowd. In the hammock lay his wife, Alice, unconscious and shriveled to a skeleton. The entourage was made up of several people from each village they had passed through along the way. Curiosity caused them to follow the crowd to see what the outcome would be. We took Alice to the house of some of our native workers, Lloyd and Martha, where I had engaged a room for her. Martha helped me spread a blanket over the grass mat and we gently laid her down.

The woman's condition looked completely hopeless, but feeling an urge to pray for her, I told Lloyd to ask all the people who had come with the woman to leave the room. We closed the door and the group of Christians knelt with me to pray. Here was a woman who needed God for her body as well as for her soul. I explained to the others that I felt God wanted to raise her up. This would not be for her sake alone, but for a testimony to all the people who knew of her case.

We prayed together, asking God to show these unbelievers that he loved and cared for them, and wanted to save them. There was no particular manifestation at that moment, but all of us had peace in our hearts as we returned to our own houses.

An hour or so later I went down with a cup of hot tea and a small dish of custard for our patient, and found that Alice was barely conscious. We fed her and prayed again. The next day had its load of responsibilities, and I didn't get to see Alice at all. Martha was looking after her and reported to me that she was improving. I supplied what food I could for her, as well as quinine for the malaria.

A couple of mornings later, while I was in the kitchen telling the houseboy what to fix for the next meal, a woman appeared in the doorway with a loaded cane jar on her head. In it were several pounds of rice, a cluster of palm nuts, and a stalk of bananas. "Good morning, Ma," she said.

"Good morning," I answered. "What can I do for you?"

Her face broke into a radiant smile. "You don't know me, do you?" she said. "I'm Alice, and I'm going home now. I stopped to thank you for helping me."

I could hardly believe my senses. Here she was, straight and tall with a load of thirty-five pounds on her head, a staff in her hand, smilingly announcing that she was off on a fifteen-mile hike through the bush for home. This, after she'd been carried in unconscious just four days before, with no human hope for recovery! The good news spread far and wide, and there was much rejoicing among Christians and pagans as well.

No words can express the delight we missionaries felt as we saw the Africans renounce their pagan worship and experience the joy of receiving Jesus as their Lord.

SEVEN

SETTLING AMONG CANNIBALS

I being on the way, the Lord led me....

GENESIS 24:27

John Yeddah and Timothy, Christian workers who had accompanied William Johnson and me on our first trip from Newaka to the Pahn tribe early in 1921, went back and lived for several months in Rhodilly among the Pahn people. When the two men returned with their families to Barroba territory later in the year to attend the annual Christmas convention, a guest came with them. He was none other than King Tho, the Pahn chief our party had met on that first exploratory trip.

We rejoiced that John and Timothy had done such effective work in Pahn country as to cause King Tho to want to come with them to the convention. But never had we seen a king so regally clad as this one.

He was wearing an old black silk top hat which had turned shades of purple and green from age, and a short, tight-fitting green cricket coat that someone in England had given us. One of the workers had carried these items on a trip back to Pahn and given them to King Tho. The rest of his attire was an old red-and-white-striped dish towel tied around his loins. From there down he was bare.

Did Your Father Know This Story?

King Tho was impressed by all he had seen and heard about Christianity during the time John and Timothy had been living in his village. And he had accepted all he had been able to understand. But he still had lots of questions.

On one occasion he said to me, "Sir, this story of Jesus—did your father know this story?"

"Yes, he did," I replied.

"And his father—did he also know this story?"

"Yes, he did."

"Then why did not your father or his father come to tell my fathers the story?" he asked in bewilderment. "I am now too old to fully understand it. But I want you to tell the story to my people—I have come here to get a missionary for them."

In spite of his unusual attire, Tho's royalty showed through clearly in his dignified bearing. He was a king. He knew it, and all who met him recognized it.

Not wanting to offend him, I respectfully told him that we appreciated his interest, but he would have to make his appeal to the missions committee which would be meeting in the next few days. He agreed to this.

Shortly afterward, all the missionaries, native pastors, and workers, and many Christians from the region gathered at Blebo for the annual Christmas convention. King Tho joined the long line of chiefs coming one by one before the field committee, each to plead for a missionary, a native pastor, or a Christian lay worker to settle in his town.

Sad to say, at that convention the committee could not promise a single one of these chiefs that they would be able to send workers to his area. One missionary had just died. Three others, including my sister

Blanche, had been sent home ill in an effort to save their lives. Each of the other missionaries still on the field already was loaded with more responsibility than he or she could successfully handle.

It was heartbreaking to watch these chiefs turn away from the committee with disappointment written on their faces. I was reminded of the compassion Jesus expressed for the needy multitudes which followed him wherever he went. He told his disciples, "The harvest truly is plentiful, but the laborers are few. Therefore pray the Lord of the harvest to send out laborers into his harvest" (Matthew 9:37-38).

The conference ended and the delegates returned to their home villages. All except one.

A King's Persistence

King Tho was not easily dissuaded. He said he would wait, and wait he did. He returned with us to Gropaka, even though we had told him at his first request that we could not leave our station. But this chief had come to get a missionary, and he had no intention of going home without one.

Every morning he would come up on the front porch of the mission, knock on the door, and ask, "Kwi Kali, are you ready to go with me today?"

Each time we told him "No," he would walk off the porch and through the yard, giving out a long, drawn-out, heartbreaking wail of hopelessness.

Finally one day he announced firmly, "I cannot go home without you. My people instructed me to bring them a missionary, and if I go back alone they will kill me. I just cannot return home unless you agree to come to Rhodilly."

For more than a month, every single morning, King Tho came to our door with the same request. He meant to have a missionary, and would not leave without one. What a contrast this daily plea was, compared to the attitude he'd shown toward William Johnson and me when we'd first met him more than a year earlier! Then, full of scorn for the foreigners, he had told us we could go sleep in the bush with the monkeys, before he finally relented and loaned us a hut.

Now he was offering an open door for a missionary to come to his people, but there weren't enough missionaries to meet the demand. How much longer could we endure his pleading and the wailing that followed?

Ruth and I prayed much, and finally concluded that God must be trying to tell us that we were more needed in Rhodilly, in Pahn territory, than in Gropaka and Barroba territory. After all, we had seen a spiritual breakthrough in our area. Some of the more mature native Christians were already proving to be promising leaders.

We conferred with missionaries on the other stations, and it was agreed that the two lady missionaries at Nynabo could separate—one remaining at the station there, and the other coming to Gropaka to carry on in our place until the new missionaries who were expected in a few months arrived. So we immediately began making plans to move to Pahn territory.

When we told King Tho one morning that we would go with him, his joy knew no bounds. Using the unique communication system of passing messages from one village to another with drums, he sent word back to Rhodilly for porters to come to Gropaka and carry our hammocks and headloads. He also sent instructions for them to build us a house to live in when we got there.

We had asked the Gropaka people to supply us with porters for the trek to Rhodilly, but they refused. They said they would carry missionaries *into* their village, but they would never carry them *out* to any other tribe. Eventually the Pahn men arrived, about fifty of them.

Ethel Bingeman, a Canadian who had been on the field a number of years and who had long been burdened for the Pahn people, wanted to go with us. When she had made satisfactory arrangements for the other missionaries at Newaka station to take over her responsibilities, it was agreed she should accompany us.

Ruth Encounters Pahn Tribesmen

Before the porters from Rhodilly arrived, I formed a small party and headed for the coast to get mail and needed supplies for moving to another village. That left Ruth and Ethel Bingeman alone on the compound when these fifty cannibal tribesmen reached Gropaka. Ruth relates the heart-stopping experience she had while I was gone:

I was sitting at my small desk in our bedroom that evening with the kerosene lamp lit, writing a letter explaining to Mom our plans to move further inland to a cannibal village. As I wrote, suddenly I felt the Lord telling me to stop what I was doing and pray. *"I'll finish my letter first, then I'll pray,"* I thought to myself as I continued writing.

But the voice was quite insistent: *"Pray now!"*

I put down my pen, knelt beside the bed and began to pray. Instantly I was aware that an almost palpable black darkness approached and was about to envelop me. I looked down at my arms and hands and saw that the darkness was almost right against my skin. It was frightening. But then I saw that a light seemed to emanate from my body that kept the darkness from touching me.

Usually I would pray with my eyes closed. But this time, as I prayed my eyes were drawn to the window above the bed. There were no glass panes, and the bamboo shutters were open. I had hung a curtain across the opening for privacy, leaving a few inches open at the top for ventilation. That narrow opening was pitch black. I could see nothing outside the window, but I felt strongly that some sort of evil was lurking just outside. I continued praying in tongues, my eyes riveted on that open space, until the tenseness in the atmosphere seemed to lift.

I knew that Ethel Bingeman was at the chapel on our compound having evening vespers with the children. Taking a lantern with me, I walked the few hundred yards to the chapel and related to Ethel what I had just experienced. We called the children to come down front and kneel for prayer. I knelt by the pulpit facing the window that was just behind the pulpit and again prayed in tongues with my eyes open and fixed on that window. Once we sensed God's peace and presence with us, we saw the children safely to bed, then Ethel and I retired for the night at the mission house.

These heathen tribesmen had come to us on order of their chief, but I'm sure they didn't completely understand why they were being called upon to carry the goods of the missionaries back to their village. During the days of waiting until the caravan was ready to embark, they sometimes got drunk on palm wine and carried on into the night yelling and chanting while throwing their knives and cutlasses into the air.

Ethel and I were keenly aware of God's protection, but we were greatly relieved when Henry got back from the coast and took charge of the situation.

The Long Trek

When the big day finally came, we started on our long, arduous trek through dense jungle. Because the forest foliage was so compact, the sun never got through. The undergrowth, a tangled web of vines, creeping plants, ferns, moss, and parasitic vegetation, at times was as impenetrable as a solid wall.

There were some sections where the porters had to put down their loads and with machetes hack a tunnel through the heavy growth. We would crawl through on our hands and knees, then the porters would drag their loads after them until we reached a place where we could stand upright.

Each night we would stop in a village along the way, our presence always creating quite a stir. Of course, in each village we had to negotiate with the local chief to obtain permission to stay overnight and also request the use of a vacant hut.

It seems that some government officials, hearing that we missionaries had made a trip deep into the interior, decided they could successfully send soldiers in to establish law and order. In a tribe bordering on the Pahn territory, government soldiers had burned a large village simply because the people would not submit to their first demands. But the tribal warriors managed to capture the commander of the frontier force, and while the town was still burning, the men and women of the village gathered around him. According to the testimony of these people themselves, they proceeded to cut pieces from his body while he was still alive, roast them in the embers of the smoldering town and eat them before his eyes.

When we reached this same village a few months later on our trek to move to Pahn country, the people had rebuilt the town and erected a new stockade around it. At the main entrance, which was well guarded by spearmen, the bones of the commander they had eaten were hanging on a crossbeam over the gateway. After being convinced by our porters that we were missionaries, not representatives of the government, they allowed us to enter the village.

One of our porters told us that the village chief was wearing around his neck a snuffbox made from one of the dried ears of the army officer. I took a picture of Ruth standing beside this warrior chief. Naturally, we had some misgivings about spending the night in this cannibal village. But the sun had already set, and we were miles from any other village, so we really had no choice.

Our New Mud Home

Finally we reached Rhodilly. The little three-room mud house the men had built for us was far from comfortable, but this was our new home. Soon the rainy season was upon us, and we discovered that the thatched roof was not thick enough to shed the torrential rain. Water came into the house and ran down the walls and across the mud floor in rivulets. We had to have workers repeatedly reroof the house until at last there was enough leaf on it to keep the rain from coming through.

The village women came again and again to beat the floors when wide cracks appeared as the mud dried out. They would sprinkle a portion of the floor with water, then pound it with a heavy crooked club, shaped for the purpose. The group worked in unison, keeping rhythm by singing or chanting a melody as they pounded the mud into a smooth surface.

At our new home children and young men continually besieged us, trying to figure out our ways of doing things. Our old-fashioned woodburning cookstove was a novelty to them, as Pahn women always cooked in a heavy iron pot placed on three large stones around an open bonfire, usually outside the house. Our bed was another unusual item, as the villagers all slept on bamboo mats on the mud floors of their huts.

One young man, Kiday, seemed underfoot all the time. He was anxious to learn, and had picked up enough West African Pidgin English for us to communicate with him, though it was a laborious process.

Before leaving Gropaka we had been warned by government officials and Barroba chiefs that the people of Pahn truly were cannibals. On arriving at Rhodilly we hardly knew what to expect. After a few weeks, during which there were no wars or fighting and we had seen no real evidence of cannibalism, we began to wonder if the reports really were true. Since Kiday seemed so open and friendly, Ruth decided to ask him outright about the matter.

Kiday was a typical Pahn man of warrior age—probably in his mid-twenties. He wore no shirt or trousers or shoes; only a loincloth made of bark beaten into a pliable piece like very rough burlap, tied around his body with a rope made of vine. His head, covered with a hundred or more tiny pigtails, reminded us of a much-used mop. His hair had been oiled with palm oil and then the finished coiffure was treated with cow dung (which killed head lice, a very common affliction).

Watching for the opportunity, one day Ruth began talking with him in Pidgin English and broached the subject of cannibalism.

"Country Fashion"

"Kiday, I be stranger for your country and I no savvy all your country fashion," Ruth said. "You fit to help me learn your country fashion?"

"I fit," he replied.

"Before I come for this town I hear long time how Pahn people, you eat somebody. It be true? Pahn people eat somebody?"

He didn't answer her right away, but spent several minutes studying her face to determine whether she was trying to trap him, or intended to ridicule him.

After waiting a few minutes Ruth said, "Kiday, it no be palaver. We come to Pahn to help Pahn people. Every people got different, different fashion. I only want to know how your country fashion be. Maybe I no hear true; I be stranger. You be friend for mission so I ask you. It be true? It no be true? Pahn people eat somebody?"

He seemed to recognize that she was truly sympathetic and serious about wanting to learn. "It be true. We eat somebody," he answered.

"You, yourself, Kiday? You ever eat somebody?"

"I eat plenty people," he replied.

"Who you eat?" Ruth asked.

"When we got some war, this side [*throwing out his right arm*] fight this side [*throwing out his left arm*]. We catch somebody from other side and chop him," he finished, grabbing at the air by his left arm and bringing his right hand to his mouth with a flourish. (*Chop* was the common word meaning "to eat.")

"Oh, I see," Ruth responded, nodding. "Then some day you go vex for me and then you go chop me?"

"Oh no, madam, you be white man!" he exclaimed.

Subsequent experience taught us that cannibalism really was practiced in that tribe. Kiday was one of the young men who accompanied me on the trek to rescue little Jitueh a few weeks later, so he was well aware of the seriousness of my predicament when I tried to negotiate for the child's release.

Soon after reaching Rhodilly, Ruth and I were stricken with malaria and were shut off from any contact with our missionary friends nearer the coast. We did not know the language of these primitive people, and most of them knew not a word of English, so it was very difficult to communicate with them. But we were confident it was God's will for us to be in this dark place. And with the help of the Lord and two faithful, godly workers from Barroba, we managed to sow some seed that eventually began to bear fruit.

EIGHT

GETA—THE SACRED MOUNTAIN

I was not disobedient to the heavenly vision.

ACTS 26:19

We found the people of the Pahn tribe much like the Barrobas—very superstitious and given to fetish worship. Like the people of Barroba, they wore fetish charms on their bodies and used them on and in their homes. However, the Pahn tribe had one big fetish above all others—Mount Geta, which they called the sacred mountain.

The stories we heard about Geta were extraordinary. The people believed it was the home of ancestral spirits which were now under the control of Satan himself. When any of their people died, their spirits were believed to go immediately to live at the sacred mountain. As these spirits were received, they said, the mountain would be covered with clouds of smoke.

On moonlit nights the people would sing and dance to the beating of drums as they called out the name of Geta, while performing peculiar contortions and gesticulations. They made sacrifices to Geta by placing food in containers on the outskirts of town. In the morning, when the food was gone, they believed the spirits had come and carried it away.

We inquired whether anyone had ever attempted to climb the mountain to visit with their ancestors. One old man told us that long, long ago some foolish people had ventured too near the mountain, and Geta sent out fire and burned them up. Others who had strayed a bit too close heard rumblings of warning and fled for their lives. Some reported seeing footprints made by Satan and his followers.

After hearing these fantastic stories about the mountain, I became quite eager to climb it to prove to the people that there was nothing to all these superstitious tales. However, since these people were easily excited and seemed ready to fight at the slightest pretext, I knew I would have to broach the subject to King Tho with caution. Any action on my part that threatened their traditions could instantly put all of us in great jeopardy.

I was especially aware of the need for discretion because of something that had happened shortly before we moved to Pahn territory. Our workers, John Yeddah and Timothy, had established a small school on the mission site, and had admitted some boys from Rhodilly. After we arrived, John told us that one of the boys had run away. He asked me to go to town with him to inquire into the matter. We had barely started to discuss the case with the elders of Rhodilly (whom we considered our friends) when suddenly, without warning, they became very angry. Seizing their cutlasses and spears, they surrounded us and threatened to kill us. They were so enraged it was impossible to reason with them.

We silently prayed for God's help and eventually managed to walk quietly away from them without receiving bodily harm. That same evening King Tho and his elders had come and begged us to overlook what some of the elders had done in their anger. Then they brought a white fowl, and after cutting its throat, sprinkled some of its blood on us and on themselves. This, they said, was to be a blood covenant between us. They were never to shed our blood, nor were we ever to shed their blood. This covenant was to be extended to include other Rhodilly people in the future, and any other missionaries who might come to live among them.

But that night I wrote this cautionary note in my diary: "This covenant affects only the town of Rhodilly, and not the whole Pahn tribe!"

We never did know why the boy ran away, or why the townspeople became so angry when we tried to investigate the matter. But it served to warn us that these people could become enraged and start a dangerous fight over the merest trifle. Our subsequent experiences with them confirmed this point.

Climbing Geta

At first, when I broached the subject with him, King Tho seemed shocked that I should even suggest climbing the mountain, and warned me of the dangers involved. Finally, after we had lived among them for a time and I seemed to gain his confidence, he reluctantly consented for me to make the ascent. But only if I promised neither to shoot at Geta nor to disturb the spirits of the departed. On the other hand, I must accept all responsibility for what might happen to me and my party. Geta might become angry and send out fire to consume us. I solemnly agreed to all his terms.

Early one morning after prayers with Ruth—accompanied by John Yeddah, a few of the mission boys, and about five Pahn warriors from Rhodilly—I headed for the sacred mountain. The small town of Mobilly was closer to Geta, so we decided to enter the jungle surrounding the mountain from that point.

We had not gone far before the young warriors from Rhodilly began to call out, "Geta, our god, do not be angry with us! The white man does not bring war or trouble, but is just coming to visit you. Please do not harm us." Meanwhile, they bit off pieces of cola nut and spit on the ground while making gestures with their hands.

As we got closer to the face of the mountain the jungle became so thick we had to use machetes to hack our way through foot by foot. Soon the warriors stopped, saying, "This is far enough for us." They urged us to turn back also before it was too late. I thanked them for their help thus far, and suggested they return to Mobilly and wait for us there.

The Vision

Step by step we cut our way until we reached the base of the mountain. On the side facing us was a perpendicular cliff, which looked almost as if it had been sliced off with a big knife. As we stood there looking for a possible route to the summit, I was suddenly transfixed in my tracks. I recognized the place! I had an overpowering feeling I had seen this spot before.

"John, I've seen this mountain before," I said to my helper.

He looked at me as if I'd suddenly gone mad or become delirious with an attack of malaria fever. He reminded me where we were, and that we were the first people ever to come this close to Geta—or at least as far back as any of the Pahn people could remember. Then the truth dawned on me.

As already recounted, I had received a call to Africa while enrolled as a student at Beulah Heights Missionary and Bible Training School in North Bergen, New Jersey. One day, during a time of intercessory prayer, there seemed to appear before me a mountain on which a large number of black people were standing, overlooking a precipice. Among them I saw a horrible-looking creature that I at once took to be the devil. With a look of fiendish glee, he seized these poor people one by one and threw them over the precipice.

As I watched this vision I began to weep. "Dear Lord, isn't there someone to warn them to get back and escape the clutches of this horrible creature?" I prayed.

The answer came back, *"There is no one to tell them. Will you go?"*

"Yes, Lord, I'll be glad to go if you will just tell me where," I replied.

It was shortly after this experience that William Johnson came from Liberia to visit the school and told of tribes in Liberia's interior that had never once heard the gospel. I had responded to the call, and God had brought me this far. Now here I was, looking at the very mountain God had shown me in a vision a few years before!

The experience was so incredible that I felt on the verge of collapse with physical weakness. And my spiritual alarm bells were ringing. Were we on the devil's territory? Did he really live here? Was the mountain inhabited by evil spirits? Since coming to Africa I occasionally had felt the powers of darkness so strongly that it was almost overwhelming. But this was a new and even more intense experience.

All at once the Lord seemed to make it all clear to me. The devil not only "lived" at Mount Geta, but as a roaring lion he went about everywhere seeking whom he might devour (see 1 Peter 5:8). He was taking advantage of the superstitious fears of these primitive people for whom Christ had died, and for generations had kept them in bondage to fear. God had brought me here to proclaim the good news that Christ came to deliver them from such fear.

Sensing that God's presence was with us, our small party made our way to the top of the mountain, where we sang some hymns together. I thanked God for bringing us safely to the very place of my vision, and prayed that God would help us to reach the Pahn people for him.

After picking up some sample pieces of minerals, which were plentiful on the mountain, we returned to Mobilly. We found the men we had left behind, along with most of the townspeople, standing outside the village. They were watching to see what would become of us.

When we returned safely, some insisted that we could not have reached the mountain, or we would have been killed. Others said the devil was afraid of the white man and either hid or ran away. But the Africans who had accompanied me insisted that indeed we had reached the summit, and we produced pieces of ore to prove it. This evidence caused most of the people of Mobilly and Rhodilly to accept our testimony.

"We will now listen to the message of the white man instead of the stories handed to us by our forefathers," the people said. The young people seemed especially eager to listen to us.

News of the event spread far and wide, even to other tribes who regarded the mountain as the strongest fetish in the whole country. A white man and his party had climbed to the summit of Mount Geta and survived, and brought back samples of ore. So wherever we went after that we had no difficulty in getting an audience. Little by little the power of fetish worship was broken. Today there are Spirit-filled preachers and congregations among the Pahn people.

Mount Geta—Thirty Years Later

In 1951, R.G. LeTourneau visited Liberia in the interest of securing iron ore for the manufacture of his big earth-moving machines. By that time the mission had cleared an airstrip near the base of the sacred mountain, not far from the site of our first mission station. A small missions airplane with a pilot was placed at the disposal of Mr. LeTourneau and his geologists and engineers while they analyzed the mineral content of Geta.

LeTourneau found the mountain very rich in minerals, including iron, tin, manganese, gold, and other material. It is believed that at one time it was an active volcano, which could account for the stories about smoke having been seen on its summit in days gone by.

When we lived among the Pahn people we noticed that there were native blacksmiths who made their own iron in crude smelters and beat it into implements such as spears, cutlasses, arrows, knives, axes, and hoes. This seemed to be the only tribe in the interior who were able to do this. Cut off from the outside world, they managed to survive without importing modern tools.

LeTourneau's men asked some of the old Pahn men what they did for lime in their smelters. They reluctantly admitted that they had used human bones for this purpose. This may have been one reason for the practice of cannibalism in earlier days.

NINE

THE RESCUE

The angel of the Lord encampeth about them that fear him, and delivereth them.

PSALM 34:7

It was March 1922. We had been among the Pahn people not quite two months. A small group of Christian workers whom we had brought with us from Barroba territory were returning from a preaching trip when they nearly stumbled over a woman's body lying beside the trail just outside one of the villages where they'd had a meeting. They carried her almost-lifeless form to our mission, where she was prayed for and cared for until she revived sufficiently to tell her story.

She was a native of the Kru tribe on the Liberian coast; her name was Jetu. Misfortune had overtaken her there when her firstborn son, about five years old, was kidnapped and killed one night by witch doctors. The cannibals ate the boy, and portions of his body were used in making fetish medicine. Jetu's next child was a girl, born in 1911. During a time of famine, fearful lest some harm befall her little one, Jetu took the little girl and ran away from her husband one night and headed for the interior. For several days she followed groups of travelers until she felt sure she had outdistanced the evil spirits that might have caused the death of her firstborn.

In the strange land of the interior, she sought food and shelter for herself and her child. Finally an elder in the council of one of the Pahn chiefs offered to lend her enough seed rice to sow a small field if she would turn the child over to him for security. An agreement was made that as soon as harvest was over, Jetu would return the seed rice with interest and receive her little one back again. However, when harvest time came, the crafty old African refused to return the child, knowing he could either add her to his already large harem or sell her for a good price to someone else.

Jetu begged and pleaded in vain for the release of her daughter. One night she managed to rescue the girl and started out on the long journey back to the coast. But it was not long before she was overtaken by a band of men sent after her by the chief's elder, who beat her severely and took the child from her. Three times she made the same attempt with the same results.

Discouraged, Jetu joined the harem of a Pahn native and later became the mother of a baby boy, Bamwe. Soon she took to wandering again, and contracted an incurable disease, which left her weak and almost helpless. No one wanted her. She had been driven from one village to another until, at the village near where our Christian workers had found her, her baby boy was taken from her and she was thrown out for the wild animals to devour.

One of our native preachers was a Kru man who recognized the tribal markings on Jetu's face, and he talked to her about the Lord in her mother tongue. He warned her that she was facing eternity without God, and urged her to repent and live her remaining days for God. With diseased body and sin-burdened soul, she surrendered to the Lord and was gloriously saved. Our first convert in Pahn was a Kru woman from a coastal tribe.

Shortly after her conversion, Jetu sent for Ruth and me and pleaded with us to rescue her two children. She said she wanted them to grow up in the mission and serve the same Christ that she had found. Without too much difficulty we were able to get her boy, Bamwe, returned to her, since we were acquainted with the chief of the village where he had been taken. However, the hope of recovering the little girl was quite a different story. We told Jetu it would be almost impossible to rescue her daughter, as she was held captive in a village three or four days' journey from our mission, which was under the supervision of a different paramount chief. This chief and his people had lately been at war with our section of the tribe, a situation that had resulted in much bloodshed and ill feelings.

The people of this distant village had never seen a white man nor come in contact with outside civilization. Knowing they were suspicious of strangers, we hesitated to go among them on such an errand. But Jetu would not take "No" for an answer. Her lament was always the same: "Oh, if I could only see my daughter again before I die."

After days of listening to her pitiful pleading, knowing her time on earth was short, I decided to do what I could to fulfill her wish. After much prayer and deliberation, I organized a group of workers to go with me on this errand of mercy. Meanwhile, Ruth, Ethel Bingeman, and the Christians at the mission prayed that God would prosper our journey.

Our little caravan set out one morning just before dawn. Fortunately, some of the young men from our village who had been persuaded to accompany us previously had seen Jetu's little girl, Jitueh, and would be able to identify her when we reached the village of her captors. The trail was long and difficult. At times we had to skirt certain villages because of the recent hostilities, which only lengthened the journey. At other times we entered villages walking between rows of warriors whose spears were raised in a menacing manner. But God was with us.

On the third day of our long march I was stricken down with fever in the middle of the dense forest. When our supply of drinking water was spent, my tongue became swollen and my lips parched. But we continued the trek despite my high temperature, as there was no place to stop for rest. Finally, I fell exhausted by the side of the trail and lost consciousness.

My faithful African pastor, John Yeddah, who joined me on this trip, had seen other missionaries die. He thought my time had come. He and the other Christians in our party gathered around my seemingly lifeless body and prayed desperately for me. We were miles from any village. It appeared that my name would be added to the long list of those who had lost their lives trying to open up Africa to the gospel.

Meanwhile, my father, living on the family farm in South Norwalk, Connecticut, was awakened from sleep in the middle of the night with a burden to pray for me. God gave him a vision of me lying there on the trail in the African jungle, burning up with tropical fever. Kneeling beside his bed that cold March night in Connecticut, he prayed and interceded for me for some time, until he felt the assurance that God had answered his prayer. In fact, in his vision he saw me get up from the path and struggle on.

How long I lay beside the trail I do not know. But suddenly, to the amazement of those who traveled with me, I regained consciousness, stood to my feet, and was able to continue my journey. God gave me supernatural strength for the ordeal that lay ahead in the rescue of little Jitueh.

Months later we received a letter from my father telling of his unusual experience. Upon comparing notes we found, allowing for the difference in time zones on the two continents, that his vision and subsequent intercession for me occurred at exactly the same time that I had been stricken with fever. God heard my father's prayer and raised me up to continue on my way. I am confident that my ministry was extended an additional fifty years as a result of the intercessory prayers of my dear old dad.

Finding Jitueh

As we approached the village where Jetu's daughter was held captive, we prayed that God would go before us and work things out for our good and his glory. On entering the village, one of my carriers spied Jitueh playing with some other children. Without being noticed by any of the villagers, he pointed her out to me.

When we proceeded directly to the home of the chief, it was quickly noised abroad that a strange party of travelers had arrived and a crowd soon gathered. After exchanging the customary greetings, which are long and very ceremonious in Africa, we assured the chief that we had come peaceably. However, he and his elders eyed us with great suspicion, and I realized that almost every man in his circle was armed with a weapon of some kind.

Knowing that there was more or less a state of war existing between these people and those in our section of the Pahn tribe, we felt it would be safer to spend the night elsewhere. So I told the chief my visit would be brief this time, but that I hoped to return in the near future and tell him and his people more about the good news of salvation.

Praying for wisdom and trying to be tactful and diplomatic, I began by inquiring whether any of them happened to know a wandering Kru woman by the name of Jetu. They all looked blank and denied having ever heard of such a person. I continued by telling them that Jetu was at our mission in a dying condition and was begging to see her little girl before she died. I explained that I had promised the dying woman to do my best to find the child and, hearing that she was in their village, had come to seek their help. I appealed to the kindheartedness of the chief, suggesting that I was sure he would be deeply touched by the dying mother's plea, as I had been.

Reluctantly the chief admitted that he had known the woman; her child had been in the village at one time, but had left a few days before with another woman for parts unknown. Otherwise, he said, he would have been only too happy to send the child to see her mother. Then I told him I knew that Jetu's daughter was still in his village and pointed her out to him.

The people looked at me in amazement. One said, "The white man has plenty of sense." Fearing they might whisk the little girl away and that we would never see her again, I requested that they bring her to the palaver circle where we were gathered. This they reluctantly did. When Jitueh arrived, I smiled at her and asked if she would like to see her mother. She didn't answer, probably out of fear. But her big brown eyes looked up at me pleadingly and seemed to say, *"Oh, I surely would!"* I felt then and there that I could not leave without her.

I asked the chief to allow her to go with us to see her mother, or if he wished, he might send along one of his trusted servants to look after her. I had a feeling that if we could once get her to our mission station, we could somehow negotiate her release. But the chief denied my request.

Next, I asked the chief if he himself would accept my invitation to return with us for a royal visit to our mission, and bring the child along with him. This proposal also was turned down. Then I offered to redeem the child by paying to the man who claimed to own her the price of a full-grown woman. When this was refused I offered to pay the price of two women, and then three. I felt that no price was too great to pay if only Jetu could see her daughter once again and know that she was safe in the mission before she died.

After talking the palaver—which lasted for several hours—without success, I suddenly decided to take desperate action. I told them that owing to the lateness of the hour I would have to leave. Because they did not see fit to accept any of my proposals, I would just take the child with me and be gone. Then, if they wished, they could follow me in a few days to our station, where we could further discuss the matter.

So saying, I handed the little girl to one of my men to carry in his arms, bade the chief and his elders farewell, and quickly left the village. The people parted and made a way for us through their midst, but immediately showed their displeasure by the customary grinding of their teeth.

We were hoping for the best, though we were hardly prepared for the worst. But we knew for sure that we needed to put as much distance as possible between us and the village and try to reach home before Jetu died. Despite our late departure because of the lengthy palaver, we managed to make three towns before sundown.

Arriving at the third town, we asked the chief for a place to stay for the night. He gave us a large hut overlooking the village courtyard where all trials were held and all palavers discussed. We conducted a brief service there and presented to the townspeople the first gospel message they had ever heard.

God's Protection

Following the meeting, the chief instructed his head wife to prepare a tasty meal for his guest, the white man. Shortly she appeared with a calabash of cooked rice and an earthen bowl of rat soup cooked with palm nuts. The woman tasted the rice and the soup in our presence to prove that the food had not been poisoned. The carrion rat meat made it taste like poison to me, but the abundance of red pepper used in its preparation helped to cover a "multitude of sins." I had been told that if the guest of a chief in that tribe refused to eat the food set before him, the woman who prepared it would be killed as a witch.

Therefore, to save the poor woman's life, I prayed, "Dear Lord, sanctify the food and please don't let it kill us." It didn't!

It was customary for our carriers, when on trek, to spend the night scattered about in various huts throughout the village. But that night all of them were very anxious to stay in the same hut with me. After committing ourselves to God's watchful care, we prepared a place for Jitueh to sleep on a mat next to my cot, and turned in for the night.

About midnight I was suddenly awakened by the sound of beating drums and bloodcurdling screams. Arising from my cot, I looked out through the only opening in the hut, a small doorway facing in the direction from which we had come earlier in the evening. To my consternation I saw a mass of black humanity pouring through the north gate of the village, screaming and yelling at the top of their voices.

Each one carried a weapon. And I could understand enough of the language to realize they were shouting, "Where is the white man? We have come to kill the white man! We know he is in the town and if you don't tell us where he is, we'll burn your town to the ground!"

I saw one of the frightened townspeople point to the hut where we were staying. That was all the signal they needed; they made a mad rush in our direction. Their wild cries awakened John Yeddah and the rest of our party. I can almost see dear old John yet, as he came over to the opening and knelt beside me. "Look at them!" he said. "Did you ever see such wild people? Do you hear what they are saying?"

"Yes," I assured him, "I hear altogether too well."

As we watched they halted in the middle of the open space before us, where there were several human skulls, an elephant skull, and a huge rock which was used by the people for a whetstone to sharpen their hunting and farm implements. We saw these men sharpen their weapons on the stone and take an oath. It was the strongest oath in the tribe, which included drinking their own urine from their hands and vowing that they would neither eat nor sleep until they had killed and feasted upon the white man.

John turned to me with tears in his eyes, saying, "Mr. Garlock, what shall we do?" I replied that there was only one thing we could do, and that was to PRAY. And pray we did. Our little band poured out their hearts to God. We certainly did not search for flowery words, but cried out for God to have mercy upon us and help us.

I remember asking the Lord to forgive me where I had blundered and done the wrong thing, to overlook my ignorance and in his mercy help us out of our predicament. I reminded the Lord that we believed we had come in his will in response to a dying woman's prayer—and that my wife and the other Christians who were praying for the success of our trip would never know what happened to us if we fell into the hands of this bloodthirsty mob.

The Angel of the Lord

Suddenly the Scripture in Psalm 34:7 came to me: "The angel of the Lord encampeth round about them that fear him, and delivereth them." As I prayed I felt impressed to go outside the hut and face the angry horde. When I told John of my plan he begged me to stay inside, and offered to go himself and try to appease the infuriated mob. He said if they killed him it didn't matter, but I must not go out there—and this brave man meant it with all his heart.

"John, I'm the one they want, not you," I said. "You and the others just continue to hold onto God in prayer."

I stepped out into the opening while little Jitueh and all my porters stayed hidden inside the hut, frightened almost to death. John came to the doorway to try to help me with the language. It was a beautiful moonlit night, and these wild men immediately saw me. Of course I could see them all too clearly.

The mob rushed forward and soon surrounded the hut. I tried to talk and reason with them, but it was useless. They had been drinking palm wine and had worked themselves into a drunken, angry frenzy. As was the custom, these men had each of their front teeth filed to a sharp point, and their hair braided into long, woolly pigtails. Their faces were painted with war paint and their quivering bodies were greased with palm oil. Their long knives and cutlasses gleamed in the moonlight.

When I saw they were too wild to listen to reason I mustered my courage and said, as calmly as I could, "You have taken your vows and made your threats, but I am trusting in my God to protect me."

They made a mad rush toward me with drawn knives, shouting, "Kill him, kill him!" The leader lunged at me with his cutlass raised to behead me. When it seemed the end had come and my head was about to be severed from my body, I closed my eyes and committed myself to God, repeating over and over again that one name that is above every name, "JESUS, JESUS!"

Suddenly there was a deathlike stillness. The tom-toms stopped beating and all screaming and yelling halted abruptly. The silence was almost palpable. After what seemed like hours, I cautiously opened my eyes—and wondered whether I could believe what I saw! Before me stood some of the men with their weapons upraised ready to strike, while others held drawn knives by their sides. But all of them were frozen in their tracks, including my would-be executioner. They stood motionless, without a sound.

The God that closed the lions' mouths in Daniel's time had held these wild, angry cannibals at bay (see Daniel 6:22)! In answer to our prayers, we saw God do what reasoning and persuasion could not do.

The Palaver Settled

Riveted to the spot, I waited breathlessly to see what would happen next. Presently the men began to relax, then they slowly backed away and withdrew to the center of the village around the great rock where they held a hurried consultation. After some discussion the leader came toward me, bowing to the ground at intervals as he came. I was still standing in front of the hut as though in a dream. This man seized me by the ankles and began pleading with me to have mercy on him and his men and spare their lives.

"We see that the white man's God fights for him," he said. "If you will forgive us we will accept your terms for settling the palaver."

I told them we wished them no harm. Since they were ready to come to terms, we would be glad to pay them the price of little Jitueh's redemption so that she might be free to return to her dying mother. When they readily agreed, we measured out to them several yards of blue trading cloth, a supply of salt, and other commodities amounting to the price of a full-grown Pahn woman. In addition to this I gave them a blanket as a gift to their chief and some trinkets for the young men who would be carrying the loads back to the village.

After accepting the goods, for which they thanked me, their leader shouted out an order. They resumed the beating of the tom-toms, and with a mad rush, disappeared into the African night. It was not until the noise of yelling and drumming had died away in the distance that I fully realized what had just happened.

I still do not know what those drunken men saw that night, but I have often wondered if they saw the angel of the Lord, as mentioned in Psalm 34:7. Or perhaps, like Elisha's servant of old, they saw the horses and chariots of fire encircling our little company (see 2 Kings 6:16-17). But one thing is absolutely certain—they did see and feel something that caused them to know God was there, protecting his servants. God had performed a miracle before our very eyes.

We spent the rest of the time until morning praising and thanking the Lord for his marvelous deliverance—there was no more sleep for any of our little party that night. At daybreak we continued our journey homeward. A couple of days later there was great rejoicing at the mission when Jetu and little Jitueh were reunited. That very night Jetu died, but God had mercifully spared her life to see the liberation of her child.

On our way back to the mission station I gave Jitueh the English name of Ruth, after my wife. I estimated she was about eleven years old at the time. She had a heavy brass ring fastened around her neck, denoting that she was a slave, which we pried off as soon as we reached Gropaka. My wife immediately began making her some pretty little dresses, and she became like one of the family. Ruth taught her how to read and write and to do small chores around the house, and at an early age she gave her heart to the Lord. How little Ruthie's face would shine as she testified in our services of how Jesus had saved her soul. She called us Father and Mother, and was my wife's shadow almost day and night.

TEN

SAVING A KING'S LIFE

For the dark places of the earth are full of the habitations of cruelty.

PSALM 74:20

One morning in April 1922, an excited, perspiring African runner came bounding up the path to our mission station. He was probably in his early teens. His hair was in long, braided pigtails, resembling a dustmop, and he had sharply pointed front teeth, and was completely naked. I could see by the terror-stricken look on his face that something was terribly wrong.

"Kwi Kali, Kwi Kali," he shouted. "Come quickly. They are about to kill your friend, King Karlo. You must try to save him."

King Karlo was the chief of a nearby village. We had visited his village a few times on preaching trips and he had listened attentively to the story of salvation. He was a good friend of King Tho and frequently visited Rhodilly. But now he was in trouble. His brother, a very old man, had died a few days previously and the tribespeople were accusing the chief of killing him through magic. Like so many groups in the area, this tribe believed that no one ever died of natural causes, but as a result of witchcraft or the evil eye.

As soon as word got out that Karlo's brother had died, every man in the community exceeded himself in expressing grief—even to the extent of rubbing red pepper in his eyes. They did this to divert suspicion from themselves. The mourning and wailing and screams of grief would sometimes keep us awake for many days and nights until the witch doctor chose a "culprit" to be tried by the ordeal of the poison cup. In those days it was estimated by some authorities on Africa that throughout the continent, no less than four million natives were needlessly killed annually in this manner.

The Poisoned Cup

After several days of witch hunting, the powerful witch doctor had named the paramount chief, King Karlo, as a suspect. Believing in the infallibility of the witch doctor, Karlo's own sons and family members had resorted to torturing him, hoping thereby to extract a confession. When I heard this I knew it would not be long until the witch doctor would insist on submitting the chief to the fearful "sasswood test." This meant he would be compelled to drink the poisoned cup. And somehow no one ever seemed to vomit the poison and be declared innocent.

Hoping to be able to rescue the apparently doomed king, I hurriedly made up a small party of local men and set out on foot through the bush for Karlo's village. Upon arriving I approached the king's compound and learned from some of his servants that at the instigation of the witch doctor his own family members had seized him. They had bound him with tie-tie vine and placed him in the attic-like storage space under the roof of his own large hut. A fire had been kindled in the center of the mud floor, and a large quantity of dried red peppers placed on the fire. For three days and nights he had been smoked with pepper fumes.

In a weakened, half-dead condition, the chief had been taken down from the loft a few hours before my arrival. He was at that moment in the hands of the witch doctor, the sub-chiefs, the elders, and tribal warriors, who were fully convinced he was responsible for all the recent deaths in the tribe. Karlo had consistently maintained his innocence to no avail. The witch doctor and his own elders had taken him to a large grove of mango trees at the edge of the village where court trials and cannibal feasts had taken place for as long as any of them could remember.

When we reached the place we found a large crowd of excited people gathered in a great circle. Karlo's semiconscious body was lying on the ground near the center. The witch doctor, a hideous-looking man, was pacing back and forth in the middle of the circle. His long mop of hair was smeared with palm oil and cow dung. His face had deep tattoo scars. A string of leopard's teeth hung about his neck, and from his waist hung pouches of juju and fetish medicine. The white tails of several bishop monkeys tied to a strap of leather around his waist trailed behind him.

"Clumsiness" Saves the King

Addressing the assembled crowd, the witch doctor was calling out the names of those who had recently died—according to him, because of an evil eye cast upon them by the chief. On the ground near King Karlo I saw a pot of sasswood and knew he would soon be forced to drink it. What could I do at this late hour to save his life?

Acting on impulse, I made my way to the center of the circle and before anyone realized what was taking place, I "stumbled" over the pot of poison, spilling its deadly contents onto the ground. My sudden appearance and my awkwardness caused no small stir among the people. I apologized for interrupting their conference by trying to explain that I had come to invite my friend, their kind and respected chief Karlo, to accompany me to my home for an extended visit.

At first it appeared that I had made a fatal mistake. Almost instantly our little company of men was completely surrounded by a solid wall of angry warriors. They were all armed with weapons—bows and arrows, long spears, cutlasses, and one or two muzzle-loading guns. Suddenly someone shouted, "Kill the white man!" This cry was taken up by others until it became a deafening roar.

Very quickly they worked themselves into a frenzy and were quivering from head to foot with almost uncontrollable rage. It now appeared that instead of being able to save Karlo, our small group would be killed along with the chief by this angry mob.

Pandemonium continued for what seemed to me like hours. They became so hoarse from shouting that some of them could hardly speak above a whisper. I was personally unarmed, although two of my porters carried guns—a shotgun and an old army rifle, which we used to supply game while on trek.

I had cautioned the bearers to be very careful when using the rifle. I pointed out to them the manufacturer's claim that one shot from this gun was capable of killing twelve men, if all stood in a row as in a platoon of soldiers and were hit in a vital spot. I did this to avoid anyone's using the rifle on small game, especially near gardens and villages where someone could accidentally be killed before the bullet was spent.

What Changed Their Minds?

If it were not for the seriousness of our predicament, it would have been hilarious to see the way my gun-bearer, Sido, clung to the old army rifle. As far as he was concerned, it could have been a cannon. We realized that, barring a miracle, we would soon be killed by these angry warriors. Fervently we prayed for divine intervention. When it appeared that the situation was completely hopeless, there came a sudden stillness over the crowd. The witch doctor, who had been in conference with the tribal elders, had an announcement to make.

He came forward and officiously declared that the elders had now decided to allow us to take Karlo to our station for a visit. Then he quickly left the grove. This sounded to us almost too good to be true. In fact, we were afraid we had misunderstood. Still fearful they might change their minds, we hurriedly placed the helpless chief in my hammock and made our way through a gap in the otherwise solid wall of warriors, and quickly left the village. What had happened? What changed their minds?

It was not until we made camp that night that I learned the real reason for the sudden, conciliatory attitude of these otherwise hostile people. In the midst of the deafening cries of "Kill the white man," Sido had slyly volunteered the information to one of the leading elders that one of the white man's guns was capable of killing twelve men with a single shot! And in addition to the bullet in the chamber it carried five more in the magazine, each capable of doing the same thing.

Upon hearing this unsettling news, the elder had called the witch doctor and some of the others aside for a consultation. They quickly decided it might be best to call a truce. In their superstition and ignorance about firearms, they apparently believed that if the gun were to be fired, it would instantly kill at least twelve persons!

Ridiculous? Of course. But God turned their superstitious beliefs to our deliverance. It took several weeks to nurse Karlo back to health. As soon as he was physically able, he attended all our daily services at the chapel and sat under the influence of the gospel. We prayed with him daily, as did our Christian workers, and he seemed to respond the best he knew how.

After he regained his strength I called a conference in his town of subchiefs and elders and managed to get him reinstated as paramount chief. He held this position until his death some months later.

Twenty-five years after we had lived among the Pahn people, I visited the tribe and found that cannibalism and the use of the poison cup had officially been abolished. Churches, schools, and medical clinics were in evidence. The influence of the Christian gospel had wrought a tremendous change among these people since the day God rescued a king.

ELEVEN

BEFORE WE KILL AND EAT YOU

But when they arrest you and deliver you up, do not worry before-hand or premeditate what you will speak. But whatever is given you in that hour, speak that; for it is not you who speak, but the Holy Spirit.

MARK 13:11

Before our coming, the Pahn tribespeople of Liberia among whom we were now living had rarely seen a white person or heard the name of Jesus. We labored diligently to give them the Christian gospel. But only a few months after arriving in this remote area, we were completely cut off from routes to the coast by flooded streams and marshes. Supplies were low, and our stomachs soon rebelled against the steady diet of rice. Ruth, especially, had problems assimilating what little food we could find.

With severe attacks of malaria fever we both became desperately ill. After weeks of pleading with some of the tribesmen to make up a caravan to go after mail and supplies for us, I finally connected with a group of men who agreed to make the one-hundred-mile trek to the coast. Ruth was so ill she had been only semiconscious for seventeen days, and did not even know when the carriers left at cock's crow one morning.

But at about midday, to my surprise, the head carrier reappeared in our doorway. I started to rebuke him for breaking his promise when he blurted out what had happened.

During a previous intertribal feud, the people of a certain village had ended up one man short in their conflict with a rival village. Typically, any enemy tribesmen who were captured during a war would be killed and eaten by their captors. Without realizing the situation, my head carrier had employed a young man, Kuso, from the side that had killed the extra man. When our party of carriers tried to pass through the village of the side that had come up short, someone spotted Kuso and recognized him as an enemy. Determined to even the score, the warriors of that village seized Kuso, beat him severely, and held him prisoner. Though the other carriers tried to protect him, they were outnumbered. Finally, they abandoned him to his captors.

When the head carrier, who had escaped and returned to Rhodilly, told me what had happened, I told him to go back to the village and demand that the chief release the victim.

"Not me," he said. "I barely escaped. All the porters are being held, and none dare leave the village. If you go with me, I will go. But never will I go back without you."

Another Rescue Mission

I hated to leave Ruth in her illness, but because we needed supplies so desperately, and because the man's life was at stake, Rachel Yeddah and Timothy's wife, Mabel—two dedicated Christian Barroba women—said they would gladly care for "Ma" while I was gone. So I hurriedly made up another caravan and started out. Just before dark we arrived at the village.

All the villages of this region were enclosed by high, wooden pole fences and usually guarded by spearmen all around. We circled around the stockade to a point as close to the prison hut as possible without being seen. I was helped over the fence by my men, whom I told to enter through the village gate and head for the prison hut as soon as they saw me enter it. Cautiously moving in the shadows from hut to hut, I came to a wide clearing in front of the chief's court and the prison hut.

The door of the prison hut was guarded by two stalwart warriors armed with spears. I must confess I was almost paralyzed with fear. And I was still weak from the effects of malaria and our lack of adequate food. Mustering all the courage I could, I headed for the door of the hut and saluted the guards with one of the few greetings I knew, "Tatto, tatto." Then I cut the grass rope holding the little bamboo mat door in place and entered the hut. Feeling my way in the darkness, I found the badly beaten Kuso tied to the center pole. At once he begged, "Please, white man, save me! Save me!"

"Well, I'm going to try," I answered.

I cut his cords and dragged him out the door. By this time the two guards had spread the alarm and a large crowd of screaming, yelling people was gathering in the courtyard. My men now joined me. Realizing I could never escape through the crowd, I sat down from near exhaustion on an old elephant skull near the prison hut, with Kuso lying on the ground beside me. I thought the infuriated villagers would tear me apart. My men and I were completely surrounded by the mob. I sat there and prayed, realizing that at any moment the end might come. I knew only a few words of their language, but I recognized enough to conclude that they intended to kill me, along with the man I was trying to rescue.

The Trial

It seemed to me that the confusion lasted for hours. Finally the people sat down in a great circle and ceased their yelling. The witch doctor rose from his place to present his case for prosecution. He looked much like so many other witch doctors I had encountered by this time. His oily, braided hair was plastered with cow dung; he had gnarled, ugly teeth and a face scarred with tribal markings. Around his neck was a string of leopard's teeth and from his neck, waist, and shoulders hung the usual packets of juju and fetish medicine. I think I have never seen a more evil-looking person.

He would lunge at me, making grotesque grimaces, and then draw back amid the cheers of the onlookers. Apparently he hoped to scare me to death, and he very nearly did just that! I could feel the powers of darkness so strongly about me that I was almost suffocating. Then he started a long, emotional harangue while pacing back and forth in front of me, waving the grass wand that was in his hand—evidently his symbol of authority.

I followed his speech mostly by deduction, and by occasionally picking up a slightly familiar word. He was relating the long, warring history of his people up to that night. He explained that they now had gotten even by capturing the enemy warrior, whom they were about to kill and feast upon. But this white man, a foreigner, had rudely interrupted their proceedings.

"Now," he asked, waving the wand toward the people, "what shall we do with this white man who has dared to upset our plan?"

"We shall kill and eat him, too!" they replied as with one voice.

The Spirit of the Lord Upon Me

Then the witch doctor came to where I was sitting on the elephant skull and laid the wand on the ground at my feet, indicating that I was now permitted to speak in my own defense. As plainly as if he had spoken in perfect English he was saying with contempt, "Before we kill and eat you, let's hear what you have to say."

I was on the spot. Although I could understand some of what I heard, I could not speak the language. My African preacher from Barroba knew little more than I did. We both desperately prayed that God would show us what to do. I feared to depend on uncertain interpretation with our lives at stake.

Suddenly, I began to shake. This disturbed me, as I did not want the people to know how frightened I really was. Then I realized the Holy Spirit had come upon me and the words of Jesus in Mark 13:11 came to mind: "Take no thought beforehand what ye shall speak ... but whatsoever shall be given you in that hour, that speak ye: for it is not ye that speak, but the Holy Ghost."

Now, sensing the anointing of the Spirit, I stood up. Looking around the circle of hostile people I reached down and picked up the witch doctor's wand that he had laid at my feet. I opened my mouth to speak a few words of their language by saying, "Ny lay ..." meaning, "Listen to me." And then it happened.

The Holy Spirit took complete control of my tongue and vocal organs, and from my lips poured a torrent of words that I had never learned. Although I was speaking fluently and quite forcefully, I did not understand the language I was speaking. I spoke for several minutes—just how long, I don't know. But when I had finished, silence reigned. Since receiving the Holy Spirit ten years earlier I had spoken in tongues many times, but never under conditions like these.

The witch doctor spoke privately to one of his men, who left to return soon with a white rooster. The witch doctor wrung its head off and came to me, sprinkling some of its blood on my forehead and on the wounded man Kuso by my side. Then he placed some of the blood on his own head and on the forehead of the cannibal chief of this village.

His actions told me that the situation required blood to be shed, so the blood of the white fowl had been substituted for ours! The trial ended around midnight with the witch doctor, the chief, and the village elders pleading, "Please do not harm us. We see that your God has power and fights for you. What can we do to atone for mistreating you?"

By using the few words of the Pahn language known among my carriers, and through John Yeddah's ability to communicate with a unique sign language he had acquired, we managed to make our requests known. I asked them to carry Kuso back to our station, and to feed our other carriers before they continued on to the coast. This they hurriedly agreed to do. Soon all of my men were eating heartily, and they were able to continue their trek to the coast.

I returned to Rhodilly that night with Kuso, who was carried in a hammock by some of these enemy tribesmen. After he had spent a few days at our station to recover, we sent him back to his village where he witnessed strongly to his people about what great things the Lord had done for him.

Finally, several days later, our carriers arrived back from the coast with the food and supplies that were so crucial to our survival.

TWELVE

HAVE FAITH IN GOD

So Jesus answered and said to them, "Have faith in God. For assuredly I say unto you, whoever says to this mountain, 'Be thou removed and be cast into the sea' and does not doubt in his heart, but believes that those things he says will come to pass; he will have whatever he says."

MARK 11:22-23

Our months of ministry in Rhodilly were rewarding in many ways. But through repeated attacks of fever, as well as near starvation for lack of proper food, my health was tenuous and Ruth had been reduced to a shadow of her former self. As soon as I felt she could stand the ordeal of the long hammock trip, I organized a small caravan and we headed back to Barroba territory, not knowing whether or not she would live to make the journey.

We were torn between feelings of victory and feelings of failure. Though we rejoiced over the many miracles God had done, yet our hearts were heavy at the thought of leaving behind so much that was still undone. Looking back on the decision, I think the determining factor was our simple, practical conviction that we would be more useful to God alive than dead. Of course, missionary deaths do accomplish much—both in testimony and in example. But missionary lives accomplish something, too. And we felt God's leading for us at that time and place was to serve him by living.

Relocating Once Again

God blessed our nine-day journey, which took longer than it normally would because Ruth was so very weak. Matthew, our houseboy, served tirelessly during each day's trek by carrying a fifty-pound load on his head. Then when we made camp, he would kneel beside Ruth's cot through the night, praying for her recovery. After a short stay in Gropaka, Ruth appeared to be improving slightly. But I felt her health would be much better if we were living near the coast instead of in the interior, as food supplies would be more readily available. Also, the need for missionaries to work among the coastal tribes was great.

We rested for a few days at our old Gropaka station, then made the long trek down to Garraway. From there we went northward up the coast by surfboat to Sinoe, a settlement at the mouth of the Sinoe River. We decided to locate at Tupplutown, about fifteen miles inland on the Sinoe River, and built a temporary mud and thatch house. Little Jitueh (now called "Ruthie") made the trip with us and continued to live with us as a daughter.

However, Ruth grew steadily worse. She reached the point where she could eat hardly anything at all. The mainstay of our diet was rice with very little to go with it except "palm butter," but she was getting almost no nourishment. Her system simply could not digest the rice— a few hours after eating, she would vomit it up again. I realized that in order to save her life she would have to leave the malaria-ridden country as soon as possible.

On her way out to Africa, Ruth's ship had stopped at Tenerife in the Canary Islands where she met a lovely missionary family. We had their address, so I sent them a telegram that she would be coming on the next ship north. I felt sure they would be willing to meet her and help her find a place to stay until I could join her a few weeks later. I needed to stay in Sinoe until Ruth's brother, Alfred Trotter, arrived to take over the work. I also needed to arrange for someone to care for little Ruthie until the Trotters arrived.

Neither Ruth nor I liked the idea of being separated, especially because it was impossible to know how soon and under what circumstances we would be together again. There were so many uncertainties. Would the Trotters arrive when we expected? Would I be able to get passage for myself to the Canary Islands when I needed it? Would the missionaries I had written be able to meet Ruth and care for her? The lack of communication over the next long weeks was to be agonizing for both of us. Here is Ruth's part of the story, as she tells it herself.

Ruth's Story

When it seemed there was no prospect of my getting better, Henry made arrangements with a Dutch shipping agent for my passage to the Canary Islands. As there was no regular schedule of service, the agent said that when the next northbound ship came in he would have the captain blow the whistle. From our home we would be able to hear it, and would know the ship was in port.

A few days later I was lying in bed asking God what the future held for us. The quinine we took to help ward off malaria had the effect of radically disrupting a woman's menstrual cycle—and of course it didn't provide total protection against the fever in any case. But I felt strongly that the "disruption" in my cycle was not because of the quinine tablets; I was sure that I was pregnant. As I lay there, wondering how my baby could develop properly when I had so little nourishment, I heard the whistle in the distance.

Gathering my strength, I got up and packed most of my personal belongings in a couple of suitcases, and in about two hours we were getting into a "gig"—a deep-bottomed rowboat used to carry cargo up the river. There were Henry and I and little Ruthie, and some of the mission boys to row the boat.

On reaching the agent's house at Sinoe we learned it would be a little while before we would be taken out to the Dutch freighter, so we sat in the house visiting. Ruthie was free to run and play, and she enjoyed looking at the river and the ocean. Later, when boarding time drew near, I sent the boys to call her, but they returned to say she was nowhere to be found. Of course I desperately wanted to see her and give her a final farewell hug, but the time came when I just had to get into the surfboat with Henry to be taken out to the ship anchored some distance from shore.

As we were gliding down the last bit of river into the open sea in the surfboat, I heard a screeching cry. I turned to see Ruthie running along the sandy beach at the river's edge throwing her arms up and down and screaming, "Ma-ma-way-y-y, Ma-ma-way-y-y-y!" It was a long, sobbing wail. Hot tears rolled down my face as I waved and waved my hand to her in farewell. Finally she stopped running where the river joined the sea. As I watched her waving to us until I could no longer distinguish her childish figure on the shore, I wondered whether I would ever see my precious little African daughter again.

When we reached the ship Henry helped me get into the mammy chair along with my baggage, and through many more tears we said our farewells. Then the crew lifted me aboard, and soon the steamer was headed north. Realizing how ill I was, the Dutch captain was exceedingly kind to me and saw to my comfort. He invited me to take meals at the captain's table, so I was given the best food available. And he provided his own deck chair and cushions in the choice spot on the upper deck so I could get the prevailing sea breezes in the tropical climate.

Arriving in the Canary Islands

After about a week at sea, we landed on the island of Grand Canary in the late afternoon. From there I had to transfer to a night boat to reach the island of Tenerife. These islands had been colonized by Spain, so Spanish was the main language—and unfortunately I knew no Spanish. But the driver of a horse-drawn cab who spoke a little English helped me by taking me to a nearby restaurant. There I got my supper amid the unbelieving stares of everybody within sight of me.

I later learned that no decent, respectable Spanish woman was ever seen in public without a male escort. Had I realized the standards of the culture I would have asked the cab driver to eat with me. But I think my very helplessness was my best defense—I was thin as a rail and as white as chalk. I couldn't read the Spanish menu, so the waiter just brought me a plate of food, and it was good. How wonderful to have something to eat besides rice! Then the cab driver took me back to the pier to board the night boat.

The overnight trip was uneventful, and I was looking forward to meeting my American missionary friends the next day. The boat was to dock at six o'clock in the morning, so despite my weakness I was up early and on deck with my luggage. But I searched in vain for a familiar face on the pier. Still hoping my friends would come, I waited until I was the last passenger left on the deck. *What in the world am I to do?* I wondered. But I had to get off the boat, so I started down the gangway struggling to carry my bags. Just then a friendly cab driver came up to me and said, "May I help you?"

I told him the name of the people I wanted to see and gave him their address. He drove me to what he thought was the district where they lived, but these missionaries were unknown. I suggested he take me to the American Consul. "At six-thirty on Sunday morning?" he exclaimed. "No, no, no! I'll take care of you."

He drove to a hotel, took me into the lobby where I could be seated, and told me to stay there until he returned. In half an hour he reappeared to say he had found the place I was looking for, so I again got into his horse-drawn cab. Soon he stopped in front of a brick wall with an arched gateway and clapped his hands. A young Spanish woman named Elouisa answered his call and opened the gate.

I was ushered into the living room of the house. There on the piano were family pictures of the friends I had expected to meet me. Elouisa smiled at me and vanished. In a few minutes an American missionary, Miss Mae Hiller, came into the room. She was very kind and made me quite welcome, explaining that the missionary family I was looking for had gone back to the States and she had taken their place.

She invited me to stay with her, as she had this big house. Since she was alone she had sublet much of it to a Spanish family with several children. I accepted Miss Hiller's offer and she made me comfortable.

My Hospital Ordeal

After a couple of days of rest I went to the hospital to see an English-speaking doctor, Dr. Zarolo. I gave him the record of my illness and he kept me there for several days for x-rays and observation. When I told him I was sure that I was pregnant, he scoffed at the very idea. "You are so malnourished that you are barely alive yourself," he said. "There's no way you could possibly support the life of a child."

One day I asked him point-blank what was wrong with me. He hesitated to answer, and I lost patience.

"Look, Doctor," I said, "I've been sick for a long time, and may be a long time getting over it. But I want to know—do I have some horrible jungle disease? No matter what you find is wrong with me, I want to know, and I want to know now!"

"Well I didn't want to alarm you," he said, "but you have the worst dilated stomach I have ever seen. It just doesn't function properly. When you eat, it's like emptying your plate into an old suitcase. The food doesn't digest; it just ferments until you lose it again."

"What is the answer?" I asked.

"Only surgery," he replied.

"No thanks," I immediately responded. "If I have to be operated on I'll wait until I get back to God's country!" Not only was I not willing to submit to surgery in a foreign land, but I felt it would jeopardize the life of my baby if I allowed this doctor to operate.

Doctor Zarolo insisted that I would never live to get out of the islands and back to the United States. Unknown to me, he had already wired my husband that my condition was precarious and that he should come at once. But when I so adamantly refused surgery, he wired Henry again and asked for permission to operate, as he felt that was the only way to save my life. But Henry had already left Sinoe and was in Monrovia waiting for money for his passage to the Islands, so the second wire never reached him. It was God's good timing that he didn't receive it.

I was unaware of what the doctor had done until the American Consul came to see me in the hospital one day. On seeing him, my suspicions were immediately aroused. I refused to answer his questions regarding my mission board and my finances. After he left I became fearful that this well-meaning doctor might be trying to find a way to overrule my protests in order to proceed with surgery. I was very, very weak. My vision was so impaired that I could not read, and at times I could not distinguish between persons who came into the room.

After the Consul's visit I determined I would leave the hospital. I called the doctor to my room and told him I planned to leave the following day. He did his best to talk me out of it, but I would not give in. Miss Hiller had been coming to see me every day at four in the afternoon, so I decided that when she came to visit I would return home with her.

The next day after the aide took away my lunch soup bowl, I got out of bed, sat on the chair, and scooted it a few inches at a time to reach the washstand and the wardrobe. It was a two-hour ordeal to wash, comb my hair, get my clothes and shoes on, and pack my bag. But God helped me to do it. I was too weak to walk unassisted, so I sat down and scooted the chair to the window where I could look out at the beautiful mountain scenery and wait for Miss Hiller's visit.

She was startled to see me sitting up and fully dressed when she came into the room. I had hoped the doctor would come by once again so that he would know I was leaving. But after waiting a couple of hours I decided it was time to go, so we started out of the hospital. Miss Hiller carried my bag and I clung to her with my left hand while steadying myself with my right hand braced against the wall as I shuffled along. We were part way down the long corridor when the startled doctor met us, grabbed a chair and put it under me.

"I can't possibly talk to you tonight, but come back to see me as soon as you are able," he said. Some twenty-five people were crowded into the waiting room waiting their turn to see him, so I could understand his not having the time to see me then. I remained seated while Miss Hiller went to the entrance and hailed a horse-drawn cab. Then she came back for me and my bag. In a few minutes we were back at her house.

God's Gift of Faith

Miss Hiller and the Spanish girl, Elouisa, helped me get up the stairs and settled into a comfortable bedroom. After a few days I felt strong enough to leave my bed and go downstairs to play the piano. That same day the American Consul called to see Miss Hiller about buying some of her furniture. As I sat nearby, hearing their discussion, I suddenly became aware that something strange was happening to me. I was seeing black diagonal streaks flash before my eyes every few seconds.

I excused myself and started for the kitchen—the black streaks getting wider and more frequent as I went. Just as I caught sight of Elouisa in the kitchen and called out her name, I collapsed. She called for help and everyone came running. I could hear everything going on around me, even though I did not understand the Spanish. But no matter how hard I tried, I could not move even a finger, and I could not speak for some time.

They picked me up and carried me to a bed nearby and wrapped me in blankets. Miss Hiller was quite alarmed and hovered near me all the time. Finally I was able to speak, and assured her, "I am all right."

Presently the temporary paralysis left me, but I was terribly weak. A few hours later the whole family helped to get me up the circular stairway to my room, and to bed. There I lay for six long weeks with no word from Henry, no word from home. I had been unable to write to let anyone know where I was. The house where the cab driver had finally found Miss Hiller was not the same address to which Henry had first written. But I knew I was in God's hands.

Elouisa and I had great times together, although she knew no English and I knew no Spanish. But gradually we each picked up a few words in the other's language with which we could converse, along with facial expressions, gesticulations, and pointing to objects. We got along beautifully. She cooked a vegetable soup for me every day, and once in a while a piece of fresh broiled fish.

Slowly I regained strength, and after a few weeks I could walk a short distance. Then I began to feel the fluttering movements and gentle kicks that confirmed I was indeed pregnant. I thanked God daily for this gift of life, and prayed for what I instinctively knew would be a son. Walking out into the sunshine on the upstairs terrace, I would look down at the ships in the harbor and speculate whether Henry might be aboard one of them. There were times when I wondered if I would live to see him again.

For several weeks I had been unable to read, but I kept my Bible under my pillow. Occasionally I would thumb the pages and hold it close to me as I prayed. One day I felt a special urge to look at my Bible, so I pulled it out from under the pillow and it fell open. All the print was doubled, or blurred, or blanked out except for the last four words on one page: "**Have faith in God**" (Mark 11:22). Those words stood out in large, clear, bold, black print.

Lying there, as I pondered the words and marveled at the miracle that I could read them, I caught sight of something else. To my right, just above my line of vision quite a distance away, I saw what looked like a black brick. It was iridescent and shining, with marbled streaks of gold in it. Though it was moving rapidly toward me, I was not afraid. When it reached my chest it vanished, but somehow I knew that whatever the object was, it represented God's gift of faith to me. At that moment I was filled with the calm assurance that I was healed.

Immediately I sat up in bed and began to thank God for my healing. Then I slipped out of bed and knelt on the floor, praying and crying and praising God and speaking in tongues. God had touched me and I was sure of it. After a bit, I rose to get back into bed, and became so sick, so very sick. I knew that this was the crisis moment. I felt if I didn't hold on to my healing now, I would be gone. So I had it out with the devil.

"Old devil, this is the last time you can make me sick!" I declared aloud. "I am healed! The Word says I am healed, God says I'm healed, the Spirit witnesses that I am healed, and I am healed!"

I made so much noise that in a few minutes Miss Hiller, Dona Carmen, and about six of her Spanish children crowded into the room, wondering if I had lost my mind. There I was sitting up in bed, tears streaming down my face, rebuking the devil and speaking in tongues. I assured them that I was just rejoicing in the victory God had given me, and that I was healed.

A few days later I received a telegram from Henry. He was at Grand Canary, and said he would arrive at Tenerife the next morning at six o'clock!

The telegraph company had forwarded the telegram from the address to which he had sent it. I nearly exploded with excitement. When I told Miss Hiller that I planned to go down to the pier to meet him early the next morning, she thought it very unwise and refused to accompany me. However, Elouisa was thrilled with the idea, and readily agreed to go with me.

The next morning at five-thirty, Elouisa and I walked the three blocks down to the pier and watched the ship pull up to the dock. This was quite a feat, as I had not been able to walk for several weeks. I caught sight of Henry in the crowd on the deck about the same time he caught sight of me, and he came running down the gangway.

What a reunion! And how absolutely thrilled I was to be strong enough to be walking around, and now reunited with Henry. The weeks of wondering whether I would ever see him again just melted away.

Three days later we got passage on a mail steamer to Liverpool, England, where we soon were able to get on a ship headed for New York. During the ocean voyage I suffered some seasickness, as there were no stabilizers on the ships in those days. But once I got my feet on solid ground again I could prove my healing. God had given me a new stomach and a good appetite, and provided the groceries to satisfy it! Glory be to his wonderful name!

Meanwhile, Back in Liberia ...

To continue my own account (Henry's), I was working in Tupplutown one day when a runner came from Sinoe bringing a telegram from a doctor in Tenerife which read: "Wife in critical condition; come immediately."

This was heartbreaking news. The Trotters had not yet arrived to take our place, and furthermore, I had no money for passage to the Islands. But instead of waiting in Sinoe, I left Ruthie in the temporary care of another missionary couple, and took a surfboat north to Monrovia, the capital of Liberia. Here I could better communicate with the outside world.

At Monrovia I wired to America for funds, and also sent a telegram to the address Ruth had left with me, inquiring about her. To my dismay the telegram was later returned undelivered with a note attached: "Addressee unknown." I felt this very possibly meant my wife may have died, based on the foreboding telegram I'd received from the doctor.

I found out later that Ruth had written to me at our Sinoe address, but I had already left for Monrovia before her letter arrived. Mail service in those days was very, very slow. She did not know about the telegrams, nor that I had gone to Monrovia. Neither did I know anything about her circumstances, or that the doctor was now trying to get my permission for Ruth to have surgery.

As soon as funds came from the States, I boarded a German freighter at Monrovia headed for Europe, which would stop at one of the Canary Islands. I disembarked at Grand Canary and took a night boat for Tenerife. Not knowing whether Ruth was still alive, I nevertheless sent a telegram to the address I had, advising that I would arrive at six o'clock the next morning.

When the ship pulled up to the pier I was on the deck. To my great surprise, there stood Ruth—a bit pale but smiling radiantly—with a Spanish lady by her side. The thrill we experienced at that reunion is indescribable. We both wept for joy as Ruth related to me the marvelous healing God had given her, and told me she had felt the movements which confirmed that she was expecting our first child.

Returning to the U.S.

The trip back to America was a joyous one. I saw Ruth gaining strength rather than steadily losing it, as she had been doing for so long. She was still extremely weak, but never once wavered from the unshakable certainty that God had healed her.

As soon as we reached New York harbor we went to Atlantic City, New Jersey, to be with Ruth's widowed mother. While visiting Mother Trotter we found some of the neighbors were anxious to hear reports of our work in Africa, so we began to have home meetings, since there was no established full gospel church there.

Soon the people wanted to start such a church, and urged me to stay on as their pastor. One family in the group owned some apartments and offered us a place to live. Feeling this was God's will for us at the time, we accepted their offer and pioneered the first Pentecostal church in Atlantic City.

About three months after our arrival in Atlantic City, our son John was born in January 1924. Fifteen months later our daughter was born in that same apartment, and we named her Ruth Anita. To us it was nothing short of a miracle that God gave us two beautiful children. During the days when we had been so desperately ill in the interior of Liberia, it seemed we would never leave the country alive. One day during that awful period, when we felt so forsaken and alone, I picked up my Bible and asked God for some encouragement from his Word. I opened my Bible to Psalm 128 and read in verse 6: "Yea, thou shalt see thy children's children."

At that time such a thing seemed utterly impossible, but God's promise has indeed come to pass. He gave us a son and a daughter, who with their companions have spent many years in full-time ministry. And we have seen our children's children! God has given us eight grandchildren and thirteen great-grandchildren.

In all my years of walking with the Lord I have continually proclaimed, "Blessed be the Lord, who daily loadeth us with benefits, even the God of our salvation" (Psalm 68:19). Truly, he has been utterly faithful to us.

THIRTEEN

EXTENDING OUR MINISTRY

I thank God ... that without ceasing I have remembrance of thee in my prayers night and day; Greatly desiring to see thee, being mindful of thy tears, that I may be filled with joy.

2 TIMOTHY 1:3-4, KJV

We knew it would not be fair to take our children to Liberia because of the horrible climate and primitive conditions. So we took up ministry in the States as God opened doors for us. After establishing a church in Atlantic City we later pastored the first full gospel church in Colorado Springs, Colorado. There in the lovely mountain climate we completely regained our health.

Later we accepted a call to pastor the First Assembly of God church in Wichita, Kansas. While there, in 1932, we answered a challenge from other missionaries to help evangelize the Northern Territory of what is now Ghana, West Africa. We agreed to go because we felt the climate there would be more suitable for our children. In Ghana, as John and Ruth received their initiation as foreign missionaries, Africa stamped its mark upon them as surely as it had upon us.

[*Editor's note: The Garlocks served for four years in Ghana, during which time they helped with analyzing the language of the Dagomba people. No part of the Bible had ever been translated into this dialect. They also built the first Pentecostal church in Tamale, the largest city of the Northern Territory. But they elected not to make the details of this missionary term a part of this book.*]

After returning from Ghana we pastored the Full Gospel Tabernacle in Kansas City, Kansas for seven years. But Africa was not through with us.

Revisiting Liberia

In 1923 when I left Sinoe—the last station at which we had worked in Liberia—I had left Ruth, our African daughter, with a nearby missionary until my sister Blanche and her husband Alfred Trotter arrived. They cared for her during their time of missionary service. Then, when the Trotters had to leave the field because of Blanche's health, they asked some Methodist missionaries to take Ruth into their mission school so she could complete her education. The Williamses gladly agreed.

The Methodist station was on the coast at Nana Kru—the area where Ruth had been born to Jetu. When Alfred took her there he explained to the Williamses how I had rescued the little girl from slavery and returned her to her mother, a Kru woman, and then how we had kept her as our own daughter upon her mother's death.

On hearing this story and seeing the girl, a native preacher at Nana Kru, Amos Wrubu, cried out, "This is my long-lost daughter!"

He then told Alfred the same story that Jetu had first told us about the kidnapping and murder of her son by witch doctors. He said Jetu had taken their daughter and run away, and he had heard nothing from her since that time. When Wrubu gathered the little girl in his arms and pointed to the tribal markings he had put on her forehead when she was a baby, there was great rejoicing at this amazing reunion of father and daughter. Little Ruth stayed with Mr. and Mrs. Williams at their mission school until they left for furlough, then she went to live with her father.

News From our African Daughter

During our years in Kansas City, we received a heartbreaking letter from Ruth. Somehow she had gotten an outdated address for us, and the missionaries at that station forwarded her letter to us in the States.

Ruth explained in her letter that she had written to us, her Christian parents, many times before, without ever receiving a reply. We never found out why none of those letters had reached us, but somehow this one got through. She told us of her marriage to a Methodist pastor, Benjamin Suehn, and of the birth of her four children, one of whom had died. She had named one son after me. She also said her father had died, and of course she barely remembered her natural mother, so she felt we were all she had left for a family. She closed by saying, "I beg you all, send me your comfort words from your mouth."

Although we were thrilled to hear from Ruth, we were saddened to think that all her earlier letters had been lost. Because we had not wanted to divide her loyalty to the Williamses, who were caring for her and providing her education, we had not tried to keep in touch with her. And we were unaware that she had gone to live with her father.

On receiving this word from her, however, we wrote her immediately and assured her of our interest and prayers. For the next several years we corresponded with her as regularly as possible, and often sent gifts for her and her children, as well as teaching aids for them to use in their church.

Then in 1943 we moved to Springfield, Missouri, when I was asked to become the Field Director for Africa for the Assemblies of God Division of Foreign Missions. While serving in this position I made many trips to Africa to survey the work in the countries on the continent where our missionaries were working. At the time I had the oversight of some 150 full-time missionaries. On a trip scheduled for December 1945, Ruth planned to accompany me, and we hoped it would be possible to visit our African daughter during our time in Liberia.

We wrote to Ruth and told her when we expected to be in Africa, but warned her that we were not at all certain whether we would be able to visit her town. In spite of vast improvements made in modes of transportation over the years, travel in Liberia was still very primitive and impossible to plan very far in advance.

We reached Liberia in December 1945, in time to be present at the annual Christmas missionary convention that Blanche and I had attended twenty-five years earlier. While at the convention a young native came to the guest house where we were staying to ask if we knew Ruth Suehn. We replied, "Yes, we do." Smiling broadly he told us he was from her town, Barclayville, and that he would be happy to carry a letter from us to her. So we sent word to her that we would do our best to visit her in early February 1946.

Following the convention I went on a long trek into the interior to visit several remote stations, and Mrs. Garlock went with two other lady missionaries to spend some time at the station in Newaka. For this trip one of her hammock men was the son of Gredeji, from Gropaka. The elder Gredeji had been one of her carriers on her first trip to the interior in 1921.

Journey to Barclayville

I rejoined Mrs. Garlock in Newaka on January 22, 1946 and a few days later we started out for Cape Palmas. From there we had to go fifty miles up the Atlantic coast to a town called Pickaninny Cess, and then ten miles inland to Barclayville. We had hoped to make the trip up the coast by plane, but found that air service had been discontinued. The only way left was to get a surfboat to take us to Pickaninny Cess, which was difficult to do. Finally we found a headman with a boat and crew who said he would take us; he planned to leave Cape Palmas at 2:00 P.M., January 28. But when we came back at the appointed hour the headman was nowhere to be found. We looked him up and asked why the delay.

"De breeze, he no plopla yet," he replied. (*Plopla* was his Pidgin word for "proper.") But he assured us he expected the right breeze to come up at any time, and he would let us know when he was ready to start out. (The boatmen were not keen on pulling on the oars hour after hour, so they would wait, hoping for a good breeze so they could sail quickly along the coast.)

We finally went to bed fully clothed in order to be ready to leave at a moment's notice. At 4:00 the next morning the headman came and told us, "De breeze, he plopla now." We got into the boat with our baggage and gear along with the four mission boys who had come along to help us carry the loads. In addition to our personal baggage we had to carry with us a folding camp bed and mattress roll, mosquito net, a hammock and its bamboo pole, water canteens, kerosene lanterns, wash basin, a box of groceries, eating utensils, and a sun umbrella.

It took more than eight hours to travel the thirty miles up the coast to Garraway, the town where we had had our wedding in 1921. We stopped there to rest after the tiring trip, and at 9:00 P.M. we boarded the boat again for the rest of the journey to Pickaninny Cess. Whenever the breeze quit, the men usually would take to the oars. But time meant nothing to them. If we didn't get there today—well, there was tomorrow or the next day. Why in the world is the white man in a hurry?

We reached Pickaninny Cess twelve hours later at 9:00 A.M. on January 30. After we had our gear unloaded from the boat we had a "palaver" with the boatmen. They wanted to leave again right away to return to Cape Palmas. We explained we wanted to visit overnight ten miles inland, and then return to Cape Palmas the next day. It took some time to convince them to wait until the next day to take us back to the Cape.

Then there was a palaver to get hammock men from Pickaninny Cess to help us with the ten-mile trek. We were only able to get two carriers to carry a hammock for Mrs. Garlock, which meant I had to walk all the way. The four mission boys also went along to help carry our gear.

We had never been to Barclayville and had no idea what to expect. The two hammock men were quite puzzled as to why we were going there at all. They kept telling us again and again that there were no white people in Barclayville, the mission station was empty, and no African government official lived there—thus, in their view, nobody of importance was there for us to see. We kept insisting we were going to see a black African family, but they simply could not comprehend such a thing.

The village of Barclayville was not a compact little town. It was bush country and each little house or group of houses was by itself, completely surrounded by forest and bush. Christian houses were distinguishable from the ordinary round mud huts, as the Christians had taken to building rectangular houses with two or more rooms, though they still were made of mud and thatch.

Our trail led into a small clearing where we saw two rectangular houses. Near the door of one of them a group of teenage girls was talking. When we approached and asked them if they knew where Ruth Suehn lived, they gave directions with broad smiles—it appeared they were expecting us. So we trekked on. Mrs. Garlock was carried in the hammock at the front of the line; I went behind them with my five-foot walking staff; and behind me were the four boys with loads on their heads.

The Reunion

A short distance down the trail we caught sight of another rectangular home. In the yard stood a woman leaning over a tub sorting clothes. My wife recognized that it was Ruth and called to the hammock men to stop and let her out of the hammock, but they insisted on taking her up the hill to the mission house. Finally we persuaded them to stop.

Ruth spotted us from her yard and started running toward us. She reached me first where I had stopped on the path; Mrs. Garlock was struggling to get out of the hammock to join us. Ruth did not say a word, but just grabbed me around the waist and hung on tightly. I am sure it was a startling sight to the carriers to see me, a white man six feet tall, being hugged by this short, plump little African woman. When she let go of me she threw her arms around Mrs. Garlock, the tears flowing freely.

As I looked at her beaming face I remembered that night so many years ago when God had enabled us to rescue her from slavery and bring her to the bedside of her dying mother. The emotions we felt at the moment of our reunion with her are impossible to describe. After a few moments we all relaxed and walked toward the house.

At first Ruth could scarcely talk. But after reaching the house we sat down on some benches under the wide, overhanging eaves and began to share what had happened in the years since we had last seen her. She could hardly believe we were real. She kept her hand on Mrs. Garlock for hours, as if she were fearful she would disappear if she let go of her. As soon as we sat down, her three children snuggled up as close to us as they could. She evidently had told them a great deal about us.

We sat and talked with Ruth for hours, but unfortunately her husband, Benjamin, was attending a church conference in a distant town, so we missed seeing him. During the afternoon, two of the Christian girls we had seen on the path coming into Barclayville came to the house, and without a word or sign from Ruth, began preparing a dinner of palm butter and rice.

Toward sunset Ruth and her children walked with us up the steep hill to the abandoned mission station—a tragic, poignant sight that stirred us deeply. We could see scores of mud channels made by termites over the stone foundation and into the walls. In West Africa, once a building has been abandoned, the termites quickly take over, as they had here. As we made our way back to Ruth's house we stopped to rest at a grove of coffee trees that were in bloom. It seemed such an idyllic place, the scent filling the air reminding us of the scent of orange blossoms.

On reaching the house we found our baggage had been carried into a large room, which we surmised was Ruth's bedroom. An eighteen-inch shelf about four feet off the floor went around two sides of the room and was covered with a clean white cloth. In one corner stood a double bed with a mosquito net hanging from the overhead frame. We presumed that this was where we were to stay.

In a few minutes the girls announced that "chop" was ready. Entering the dining room, we found a large native-made table set with plates and spoons for two people. Ruth told us to sit down and eat, but we insisted that she and the children come and eat with us. They were pleased with the idea, and the girls beamed proudly as they brought additional plates and served us. Mixed in with the palm butter gravy was chicken, sweet potatoes, and palm cabbage. What a treat! We had not eaten "palm chop" for twenty-three years, and evidently Ruth had warned the girls to go easy on the red pepper. It tasted just right, without blistering our tongues.

We talked with Ruth until 9:00 that evening. Our boys had put up the double camp cot in the large room where our baggage had been placed. When we were preparing to retire Ruth came into the room several times, said nothing, hesitated a bit, then walked out. Finally Mrs. Garlock said, "Ruth, what is the matter?"

She hesitated a moment and then said, "Mama, it's a long time since I slept in the same room with you and Pa."

My wife quickly answered, "Ruth, if you want to sleep in here too, that is just fine with us. You do as you want to do." She nodded and smiled and left the room. We don't know how she managed it, but after we had bedded down in our camp cot and the lantern was out, she got the children into bed with her there in the same room without making a sound.

At 5:00 the next morning we awoke to discover that Ruth and the children were already up. Not only had they dressed, but they were dressed up as if for some special occasion. When I asked Ruth the reason she said, "Oh, we are going down to the beach with you!"

Our boys helped us get our things packed up and we were ready to leave about 6:00 A.M. Ruth tied two-year-old Helen on her back, and with five-year-old Henry and eight-year-old Nancy walking beside her, she followed us out on the trail for the ten-mile trek to Pickaninny Cess. They had to almost run to keep up with the men who were carrying Mrs. Garlock's hammock, but Ruth wanted to stay alongside the hammock near "Ma." Finally we convinced her to drop back and walk with me at a more leisurely pace.

Another Farewell

We reached the beach about 8:30 A.M. and began rounding up the boatmen to get our things aboard. We found the boat already loaded with some cargo-bundles of casava fiber, large sacks of palm kernels, coffee beans, cocoa beans, and dried coconut. Also, an African woman had been taken on as a passenger.

After a tearful farewell to Ruth and the children, we stepped into the boat. Sitting at the rear, we could look toward the shore as the boat headed straight out from the beach in order to get around a rocky jetty. Mrs. Garlock was almost face-to-face with the boatman taking care of the rudder. The tears were running down her face as she constantly kept waving to Ruth and the children standing on the shore, who were waving back at us. The man at the rudder told the others on board that the white woman was crying. When Ruth raised her other hand to continue waving, the woman passenger's head came up under her arm and she looked straight into my wife's face to see if she was really crying. The whole experience of our visit to Barclayville was mystifying to these Africans.

That was the last time we saw Ruth. We couldn't help but remember the day long ago when we had left her standing on the beach crying and wailing, "Mam-ma-way-y-y ..." And now all these years later we were waving and crying again, only this time she was completely silent with her children huddled around her. Arriving in Cape Palmas, we stayed there for a few days in a mission house while awaiting a military plane on which we could fly up to Monrovia to continue our journey.

One afternoon a stranger knocked on the door and asked to see Pa Garlock. It was Benjamin, Ruth's husband. He told us he had gotten home late in the afternoon on the day we left and found Ruth lying on the bed crying. She had told him, "When my mama died, God gave me another mama, but after a while she went off and left me. Yesterday she came to see me again, and now she has left me again." He felt helpless to comfort her, but upon hearing her words he felt he just had to make the long trip to come and meet us.

From that time we kept in touch by mail. Through the years Ruth and Benjamin pastored a number of churches in the area of the Kru tribe on the Liberian coast, and he trekked countless miles through the bush during his long term as a district superintendent. Finally, when his legs failed him, Benjamin could no longer walk very far or stand in the pulpit to preach. With her zeal for God and the training she had received, Ruth was able to take over many of his responsibilities. Before Benjamin died, the Methodist bishop, recognizing her ability and godly character and faithfulness, fully ordained her to continue Benjamin's ministry.

A few years later her elder daughter died and left five children, so Ruth also took on the responsibility of rearing a second family. We were able to have a treadle sewing machine delivered to her so she could make clothing for the children.

Looking back, we could only marvel at the goodness of God and his infinite wisdom in planning a multitude of details that, in the aggregate, fulfilled his glorious purpose in the lives of so many people. Whatever risks were involved in rescuing Ruth from slavery in 1922, the results were certainly well worth it. She became a daughter of whom any parent could be proud.

FOURTEEN

THE RETURN OF KWI KALI

So then neither he who plants is anything, nor he who waters; but God who gives the increase.

1 CORINTHIANS 3:7

On that 1945-46 trip to Liberia, while Ruth stayed at the Newaka station, I planned to visit all our mission stations in the interior. Although our first missions aircraft had arrived in the country a few months earlier, there were as yet no airstrips in the interior large enough to accommodate the plane. So, after getting a group of porters together to transport my small traveling kit by headloads, I set out on foot. After my absence of more than twenty years, the old trails seemed much more difficult than they had been two decades earlier, and my pace was somewhat slower.

Yet it was a privilege to revisit this part of the country. In some ways—particularly the mode of transport—it seemed little had changed except that some of the villages I remembered had long since been destroyed.

One night as I prepared to preach, a middle-aged man came running up to me calling out, "Kwi Kali, Kwi Kali!"

When I asked him how he knew me, he replied, "How can I ever forget you? You saved my life!" Then I recognized that he was Kuso, the man who, with me, had come so close to being eaten. After he related to the congregation in detail the miraculous story of his deliverance, we rejoiced together over the thrill of seeing each other again after so many years.

A Different White Man

Arriving one evening at an interior village on the summit of a rather high hill, I sat down to rest on the thatch-roofed veranda of the headman's hut. I was exhausted, and I really felt like singing Balaam's song, "Let me die the death of the righteous, and let my last end be like his!" (Numbers 23:10).

In a short time the village headman arrived home from his rice farm with a homemade hoe on his shoulder. He looked me over and asked if I were tired.

I replied that I was very tired, as the day had been hot and the trails seemed unusually long. After offering me a drink of water, he sat down and proceeded to tell me that white people are not as strong as black people. He said that when his wife gave birth to a child, the palms of its hands and the soles of its feet were white. But after the child grew these turned darker and he became very strong.

After a bit of talk about the congenital weaknesses of white people, he commented that he had known only one exception. That was the first white man who had come to his region, the first missionary to bring the message of Christ to his people, the first white man he had ever seen. "This white man was different from others," he said.

When I asked him how this one was different, he went on to describe what sounded like a legendary person. This white man was very tall and very strong—a sort of Herculean giant. He seemed never to get tired; he could outwalk any black man in the country. He never used a hammock, "as most white people do these days," he said. Many times he would travel a two-day journey in one day. He was a mighty hunter. When he shot at an animal he never missed, and he often killed two animals with one shot. He was the first man he had ever seen who wore clothing.

I let him talk on for a while, and then asked him the name of this remarkable person. "We called him Kwi Kali," he said. "We named him after the white bird in our country."

"Where is this strange white man now?" I asked.

"Oh, he must have died many years ago—we haven't seen or heard of him in a long time," he replied. "He came here when I was a young man, and now I am getting old."

"Who do you think I am?" I asked when I could wait no longer to see his response.

He squinted his eyes and looked at me intently. Upon seeing the look of amusement on my face he suddenly exclaimed, "I think you're Kwi Kali!"

When my porters confirmed my identity to him, there was quite a celebration in town. The headman threw his arms about me and almost squeezed the life out of me as he cried, "Kwi Kali, Kwi Kali!" Then he danced about and called his family and the townspeople together. "Our father has returned to us! He has come home! This is Kwi Kali! Kwi Kali is home!"

Further conversation revealed that he had lived in a small village near Rhodilly where we had first located among the Pahn people. He had heard about me climbing Mount Geta, and he had heard me preach several times. And he had visited our Rhodilly mission station on one occasion, so he felt he knew us. After our departure from Pahn territory his village had been destroyed in an intertribal war and he had resettled as chief in this village where I had stopped on my trek.

That evening I held a service in the town and we learned there was a thriving group of Christians in the area. I realized anew that in the work of the kingdom, one sows, another reaps, and God gives the increase.

Making a Way for Others

Yes, I was "home" in one sense. But I could not stay. A hundred duties in a score of other places called me on. I have had many homes in Africa—yet it seemed I was always a pilgrim, leaving one area and starting again in a new place. I am happy to say that today there are Spirit-filled pastors and churches throughout Pahn territory.

Many missionaries have poured their efforts into Africa since I first answered the call to go to Liberia. Much has changed, of course, and most of it for the better. Cannibalism, for example, was a traditional way of life for many tribes in the 1920s. Today it survives only in super-secret superstitious rituals.

During my ten years of work as Africa Field Director I was privileged to visit almost every country on that vast continent. On one memorable journey, Ruth and I flew to Johannesburg to spend time with our son John and his family while they were operating a Bible school in Brakpan. While there I picked up a station wagon we had shipped from the U.S., and Ruth and I drove north and then all the way to Accra, Ghana on the western coast. We visited mission stations all along the way on the 5,000-mile journey and saw some of the most spectacular scenery anywhere in the world.

Looking back over the years, I have often felt that some of the missionary methods we used to employ now seem as primitive as the people among whom we used them. But they started something. And even in places where we saw only limited results, the missionaries who followed us later reaped a great harvest. How thankful I am.

It is gratifying to know that for some of them, Ruth and I helped open up the road and launch them into missions work. There is still something satisfying in being a pioneer.

Pioneers

We shall not travel by the road we make.
'Ere day by day the sound of many feet
Is heard upon the stones that now we break,
We shall be come to where the crossroads meet.

For us the heat by day, the cold by night,
The inch-slow progress and the heavy load,
And death at last to close the long grim fight
With man and beast and stone. For them the road!

For them the shade of trees that now we plant,
The safe smooth journey and the final goal,
Yea, birthright in the land of covenant.
For us—day labor and travail of soul.

And yet the road is ours, as never theirs.
Is not one thing on us alone bestowed?
For us the master-joy, Oh pioneers;
We shall not travel, but we make the road!
                                    —V. Helen Friedlaender

EPILOGUE

By John Garlock

T he story you have just read has, in an earlier version, gone through many printings in English, has been translated into German, and continues to stir interest wherever it goes. Its events from long ago remain timelessly relevant to all who exercise faith for the fulfillment of Christ's Great Commission to reach the world with the truth of his gospel. Many are the testimonies of how my parents' experiences have inspired and encouraged Christian workers all over the world.

The book was conceived and produced chiefly as a brief record of their earliest years of missions in Liberia, beginning in 1920. The few summary accounts of later times make it clear that Mom and Dad were still involved in Africa many years later.

It's not practical for me to try to fill in all the significant details of their lives and ministries since this book was written. But I share with you a few highlights of how their lives continued and ended—always connected to missions and its causes.

A Term on an "Easier Field"

When my parents resigned from leading a quite successful congregation in Wichita to go to Africa again in 1932, I was eight years old and my sister Ruth was seven. Mom and Dad felt they could take us with them because they thought we would find the Ghana climate somewhat more bearable than Liberia would have been.

For me it was a great adventure, as I was always made to feel that we children were part of the missionary team. At first we lived in Yendi, the capital of the Dagomba tribe, learned the language (more easily than the adults), and made friends with African children. One of my playmates, Amidou, was among the first converts to turn from the animism of his tribe and accept Christ as his Savior. Ruthie and I often participated in the gospel meetings where my parents preached—sometimes in places where we were the first white children the Africans had ever seen.

Conditions were primitive. We lived without a water system, electricity, refrigeration, or grocery stores. We felt no sense of hardship, but the climate took a toll. And despite taking quinine regularly, my sister and I suffered with repeated attacks of malaria. The uncertainty of tropical life became brutally clear when Guy Hickok, a 27-year-old single missionary in our party, died. He had been in Ghana for only two years, and was like a big brother to me. Beulah Buchwalter, another single missionary, often was ill also, but she took time to give me my first lessons on the trumpet.

I remember how the missionaries, six in all, would gather every morning around a table and work at devising ways to create a written form of the native language, which had never been done before. There was no alphabet, grammar, dictionary, or Bible. I was amused that sometimes there were six ways of spelling a troublesome word, because some of the sounds simply couldn't be written with English letters. In the end they used symbols from the international phonetic alphabet.

Though neither Mom nor Dad were trained translators, they had a significant part in these first efforts toward creating a Bible for the Dagomba people. Mom soon found there was no existing word to mean "the cross." The concept of crucifixion did not exist in this culture. She took two words: *dago*—anything of wood, and *pulli*—a covenant, and combined them to form *dapulli,* the word now used in the completed New Testament and in Dagomba churches of every denomination.

In 1933 our family moved to Tamale, a larger town than Yendi. Here I made more friends, improved my fluency in the language, and read every book I could find, including some borrowed from British colonial officers who governed the country. Dad found and bought a tough little dwarf horse, on which I enjoyed exploring nearby villages. Mom homeschooled my sister and me using the Calvert Course she ordered from Baltimore, but she expanded the curriculum by adding a lot of Bible study.

When Beulah Buchwalter's health problems worsened in 1935, she made plans to return to the U.S. Because my sister and I had struggled with repeated attacks of malaria, my parents decided to send us with Beulah to live with our grandmother in New Jersey while they completed the last year of their term in Ghana. In a way this was another adventure for me—a thirty-day stormy voyage across the Atlantic on a freighter. Then we had a long, long year of waiting for our parents' return.

Expanding Their Ministry

When Dad and Mom got back to the U.S. in 1936 they didn't feel God wanted them to return right away to Africa a third time. A church in Kansas City invited them to come as pastors, and that's where I spent the rest of my school years. Later, during the ten years that Dad served as Field Director for Africa, my parents crisscrossed the continent many times as mentors and counselors to dozens of missionaries in all sorts of circumstances. Occasionally they had the blessing of seeing some of the fruit of their earlier efforts that still reverberated many years later.

For example, in 1952 my father was traveling by Jeep with two other missionaries in a remote part of Upper Volta, now called Burkina-Fasso. They were headed out through the bush to a remote village called Po to preach. An article in the *Pentecostal Evangel* of October 15, 1978, tells what happened when they arrived there:

> The men inquired their way to the chief, as African protocol requires, to get his approval for the gospel service they wished to conduct. The chief, a blind man, proved friendly and listened attentively while George Flattery [one of the three] told of their mission.
>
> "Have you or your people ever heard the story of Jesus and his love for all men?" he asked.
>
> To the astonishment of the three missionaries, the old chief replied with a smile, "Oh, yes, we know it well. This whole village believes in Jesus."
>
> The white men could hardly believe what they were hearing. How had it happened? Then the chief explained: "Well, twenty years ago as a young man I left my tribe for a while and traveled into Ghana to find work. In Tamale I heard the gospel preached by a missionary named Garlock, and I accepted Jesus Christ as my Lord. I was baptized in the first baptismal service of the first church built in Tamale. When I came back to my tribe later, I shared with all my people the faith I had found."
>
> The three missionaries had expected to find a remote village that knew nothing of Christ. Instead, the visit turned into a time of rejoicing in fellowship with African brothers and sisters in the Lord!

One More Missionary Term

After retiring from the position of Africa Field Director for the Assemblies of God in 1954, Henry B. and Ruth E. Garlock served a four-year term as "regular" missionaries in Malawi, East Africa, supervising, training, and encouraging African pastors. During their last year on the field, no less than thirty-three new indigenous churches were dedicated to the Lord.

In traveling around Malawi, Dad was fond of taking with him in the car some young African minister. Usually it was Gideon Bomba, a brilliant, dedicated disciple who treated the opportunity as a sort of traveling Bible school.

As they drove along the dirt or gravel roads, they often came to a spot where two or three large stones the size of cabbages sat conspicuously in the road. It was no mystery why. Some truck driver, after using the stones to chock his wheels while he changed a tire, simply drove off and left them there. At such a site my father would stop the car, get out, and throw the rocks off the road. Time after time he did this—all over Malawi.

At first his actions amused and mystified Gideon. "Why do you bother with the rocks?" he would ask. "You aren't responsible. And they aren't bothering your car; you can steer around them."

"Yes, but think of the people who come along this road by bicycle, sometimes at night," Dad would explain. "For them the rocks could be a serious hazard. It might mean a blown-out tire, a bent wheel, maybe a fall and a broken arm. We have the daylight and the time. Let's make the road better for those who come later."

Gideon would smile and shake his head, puzzled. But before long he began to volunteer to get out and deal with the rocks himself.

After Mom and Dad finished their last missionary term in Africa, they retired. Several years after having left Malawi, they were invited to an international conference that brought together church leaders from many countries. The head of the Malawi delegation was a man named Gideon Bomba. His reunion with my father was filled with laughter, tears, and hugs.

Said Gideon, "You know, Sir, it has been many years since you and I traveled the roads of Malawi together. But Sir, I want to tell you something: I still stop and throw the rocks off the road!"

Retirement and Homegoing

In the 1960s Mom and Dad lived in Bakersfield, California—first in a small house they bought, then for a few years in a mobile home park. During this time they were frequently invited as guest speakers for missions-related events in local churches. When health problems made it difficult for them to maintain a place of their own, my sister Ruth and her pastor husband, Kirk Soper, received them into their home in San Jose, California. They greatly enjoyed the interaction with the very active Soper family of five daughters. Then, after my sister's death in 1978, my parents moved to Dallas to be near me and my family while I was teaching at Christ For The Nations Institute.

In Dallas they made many friends quickly. Students at CFNI loved to hear their stories and ask questions. Some later told me they were called to missions when they heard Henry B. Garlock teach one of my classes.

At first my parents lived in their own apartment in a retirement community, then, as Dad became more feeble, they moved into our house until he required full-time medical care. During his time with us we noticed that he seemed to become more and more aware of heaven, and less and less concerned with earth. Much of his time was spent in what we called his "prayer chair." Here he read his Bible and prayed daily for a long list of individuals and ministries dear to his heart, a process that could take three or four hours. In 1985, as I sat at his bedside, Dad graduated to his reward at the age of eighty-seven.

For the memorial service, Mom wanted to address the crowd of friends present. Recalling Dad's pioneer pattern of first reconnaissance, then settlement, she said in a strong voice, looking down at the casket, "Well, folks, this is how Henry always did it. Every place we ever moved to, he went there first!" The service was full of celebration and rejoicing over a life lived well and to the full.

Moving back to a retirement-complex apartment, Mom lived on her own until age ninety-two. We visited her there almost every day when we were not traveling somewhere. Several times she flew to California to visit her grandchildren, my sister Ruth's delightful daughters.

On one such occasion I delivered her to the Dallas-Fort Worth airport and obtained the services of a redcap to escort her by wheelchair to her gate while I went to park my car. The man had no obligation beyond taking Mom to the gate. But when I came to rejoin her, I saw that he was kneeling beside her wheelchair in tears as she led him to accept Jesus Christ as his Savior. It seemed she carried her missionary spirit wherever she went.

After she moved to a full-time-care facility her sight slowly failed, but not her humor. Ruthanne and I personally took turns reading Bible passages to her on each visit, and she often mouthed them along with us, having learned them by heart long ago.

When I visited her on January 19, 1997, Mom seemed to be in a deep sleep, with no fever and no apparent pain. But she never awakened. Two days later, at ninety-nine years of age, Ruth Eveline Trotter Garlock went to join her beloved husband and the many heavenly trophies the two of them had won together. Her memorial service was a joyous commemoration of her remarkable life.

As was the case with removing those troublesome stones from the Malawi roads, the legacy of these two pioneers is still making the road better for those who come after them.

More of the Best from
Ruthanne Garlock

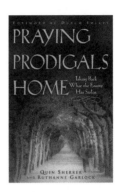

The Beginner's Guide to Receiving the Holy Spirit
The Holy Spirit and You
• How to Live in Renewal
• Removing Obstacles to a Deeper Spiritual Life
Quin Sherrer and *Ruthanne Garlock*
ISBN 08307.33930

Praying Prodigals Home
Taking Back What the Enemy Has Stolen
Quin Sherrer and
Ruthanne Garlock
ISBN 08307.25636

A Woman's Guide to Spiritual Warfare
Quin Sherrer and *Ruthanne Garlock*
ISBN 08307.35186